NUTS
A Cookbook

NUTS
A Cookbook

GREENWICH EDITIONS

A QUANTUM BOOK

This edition published by
Greenwich Editions
10 Blenheim Court
Brewery Road
London N7 9NT

Copyright © 1993 Quarto Publishing plc

This edition printed 1997

ISBN 0-86288-140-4

QUMNAC

This book was produced by
Quantum Books Ltd
6 Blundell Street
London N7 9BH

Printed in Singapore by Star Standard Industries Pte Ltd

In memory of
Richard D. Taleff,
whose love of coconut was inspirational.

ACKNOWLEDGMENTS

Special thanks to Steve Smith, without whom this book would still be just
an idea. Thanks to my family for their support and to all my friends who
served as willing guinea pigs for these recipes, particularly Martie LeBare,
Michael McEvoy, Beth and Fred Rust, Alan and Jeanette Mittelsdorf, John
Morse, my sisters Joan Rogers and Lynn Stillman and special thanks to my
mother, Ann Rogers, for the dog nutcracker.

Thanks also to Carla Glasser and everyone at the Nolan-Lehr Group.
Special thanks to Sidney Miner and Clare Wellnitz, and to Marta Hallett,
Ellen Milionis, Jill Hamilton, Tom Fiffer, Rose K. Phillips, Linda Winters,
and everyone else at Running Heads. Last but not least, thanks to Dexter
Samuel for all his help.

We would like to thank the following people for their support during this
project: the Jacobson and Ehlers families, Judy Devine for her love and
inspiration, and Maggie Jones.

Thanks also to Jill Bock, Michele Cohen, Beth Farb, Kim Kelling, Tina
Klem, Linda Winters and everyone at Jenkins & Page and 2B.

Our special thanks to those companies who generously loaned us their
beautiful wares: Ceramica, Jim Mellgren at Dean & DeLuca, Platypus,
Pottery Barn and Pauline Kelly at Zona.

Hazelnut and Honey Muffins

44

Pecan and Prosciutto Bread

46

Curried Corn and

Coconut Timbales

44

Braised Chestnuts with

Onions and Prunes

50

Vidalia Onions Stuffed

with Apples and Cashews

52

Tomatoes Stuffed with

Saffron Rice and Brazil Nuts

52

Orzo with Pancetta

and Pine Nuts

54

Barley with Wild Mushrooms

and Chestnuts

54

Sweet Potatoes with Bourbon

and Pecans

56

THREE
MAIN COURSES

Lamb in Macadamia

Cream Sauce

60

Hazelnut Stroganoff

62

Tagliatelle with

Chestnuts and Sausages

64

Grilled Salmon on

Coconut Cabbage

66

Scallops with Lemon

and Pistachios

68

Spinach Fettuccine with

Stilton and Pecans

70

FIVE
Desserts

INTRODUCTION

Nuts are seeds or fruits consisting of soft edible hearts in hard or woody shells. Popular long before scientists discovered their nutritional value, nuts were a staple in the diet of early hunter-gatherers, and archaeologists have found traces of them in prehistoric campfires. These countless aeons of nut consumption can be attributed only to one thing – nuts are delicious.

We now know that besides tasting so good nuts are an excellent source of protein as well as the B vitamins, vitamin E and minerals such as iron, calcium, magnesium and potassium. Nuts do have a high fat content, but much of this fat is polyunsaturated or monounsaturated, so eating nuts does not generally increase blood cholesterol. One exception is the coconut, which has a relatively high saturated fat level but seems, in light of its unique taste, worth an occasional indulgence.

Because fat spoils faster than starch or protein, nuts tend to become rancid if stored too long. Unshelled nuts will keep in a cool, dry place for several months, while shelled nuts, if refrigerated in airtight containers, will keep for only one or two months, depending on their fat content. All nuts freeze well and will keep in the freezer for about six months. When buying nuts in the shell, make sure they feel heavy for their size and do not rattle much. Look for nuts of uniform colour, without cracks or holes that will cause them to spoil faster.

Roasting brings out the full flavour of nuts, and most cultures serve roasted nuts solo – plain or salted. Some cuisines, particularly Middle Eastern and African ones, are more adventurous and use ground nuts as thickening agents, while Europeans and Americans tend to relegate them to snacks and delectable desserts. But nuts are much more versatile than these limited uses suggest. This book will crack open the many diverse and delicious ways of using nuts in cooking. The recipes feature the twelve most readily available and useful nuts and a brief description of each follows.

ALMONDS

Botanically, the almond is not a true nut but a stone fruit, like peaches or apricots. Almonds probably originated in the Near East, but they have long been cultivated throughout the tropics. Revered by the Romans, almonds were once regarded so highly that people believed dreaming about them would bring good luck. They came to America with Spanish missionaries en route to California – still the major American supplier – and they remain the dominant nut in world trade and the most widely grown and eaten tree nut. Where they are cultivated their blossoms serve as a fragrant herald of spring. Almonds come in two types – bitter and sweet. Bitter almonds contain prussic acid, a poison that must be leached by heating, and they are used almost exclusively for almond oils and extracts. Sweet almonds are the familiar ones used for eating and in cooking. Almonds are rich in protein, calcium and riboflavin, and most of their fat is monounsaturated. Their saturated fat content is among the lowest of all nuts.

BRAZIL NUTS

Brazil nuts, as their name indicates, originated in the tropical rain forests of South America, and they are a truly wild food. Attempts to cultivate them have met with resounding failure, and virtually all of the Brazil nuts on the market come from wild trees. They grow clustered together like orange segments, in coconut-type shells roughly the size of an adult man's head that weigh up to two kilograms. Each shell contains twelve to twenty-four nuts and is harvested from November until June by labourers called *caboclo*, who gather them from the ground after they have fallen from towering 30- to 45-metre high trees. It is not a good idea to seek shelter under a Brazil nut tree during rainstorms or high winds! After harvesting the nuts, the *caboclo* take them to trading posts where they are shelled manually. Given the highly labour-intensive method of gathering Brazil nuts – and the fact that they are 65 per cent oil and have a very short shelf life – their price is relatively reasonable. Although their fat content is one of the highest and they contain more saturated fat than most nuts, Brazil nuts are still a good source of vitamin A, the B vitamins and some minerals. Only pecans and walnuts have greater nutritional value.

CASHEWS

The cashew is an evergreen shrub native to the West Indies, Brazil and India. Today's leading cashew exporters are Mozambique and Tanzania, where Portuguese colonists took cashews and planted them. Related to the mango and the pistachio, the cashew grows hanging below a mango-like, pear-shaped edible fruit called the cashew apple. Because the cashew apple spoils within twenty-four hours of harvest, it is almost never exported, and the fortunate few who have tried this fruit say it is even tastier than the cashew nut. Cashew nuts are always sold shelled, because the cardol layer between the shell and the nut is caustic and will blister the skin on contact. The cardol is removed by heating the nuts, and the caustic liquid rendered in the process is used in more than 250 medicines, resins and industrial products. Cashews are about 48 per cent fat – almost all of it nonsaturated or monounsaturated – and they provide vitamin A, some B vitamins, iron and calcium.

CHESTNUTS

The chestnut tree is native to southern Europe and has been exported as much for its timber as for its nuts, which grow in groups of two or three in a prickly green husk. One variety grows one nut to a husk and is called a marron. Because chestnuts contain so much starch and so little oil, they are the only nut treated as a vegetable and must be boiled or roasted before eating. Further, they are sweet and soft, without the characteristic crunchiness of nuts. Low in protein and fat, but high in carbohydrates, chestnuts provide some B vitamins, vitamin E and potassium. Chestnuts will keep fresh at room temperature for only a short time, but if they are refrigerated, they will keep for two to three months.

COCONUTS

The coconut's origin is unknown, because the oceans seem to have carried it to tropical beaches all over the world. Coconut palms bear fruit throughout the year, and coconuts are a staple crop in many parts of the world. The Philippines and Indonesia are the world's chief coconut exporters. Most cultures use every part of the nut in some way: the husk woven into rope and mats; the shells formed into utensils and vessels; the flesh eaten fresh or dried to make copra – an oil used extensively in cosmetics and margarines. Even the sap is fermented to make a drink. Coconuts taste best when picked young, with greenish white skins and flesh tender enough to be eaten with a spoon. Unfortunately, they are rarely available this way, except where they grow. In the supermarket a "fresh" coconut should feel heavy, and you should be able to hear the liquid sloshing around inside. (If not, the nut has dried out.) Its three "eyes" should be dry, without any mold or rancid smell. If it smells sour throw it away! Coconuts contain a lot of fat, which, unlike the fat in other nuts, is almost all saturated.

They also contain some B vitamins and minerals. Due to its high fat content, coconut flesh spoils quickly once the nut is cracked. Fresh flesh can be refrigerated for one week or frozen for several months. Dried flakes can be refrigerated or frozen for several months.

HAZELNUTS

Chinese lore says the hazelnut is one of the five sacred nourishments bestowed on humans, and hazelnuts have been cultivated continuously in China for 4,500 years. Members of the birch family, hazelnuts grow in clusters, partially covered by a green skin. Many species grow wild in temperate areas, but only three are cultivated as a cash crop: the Turkish hazel, the Mediterranean filbert, and the Old World cobnut. The hazel is a little smaller than the other two, but once the nuts are shelled it is difficult to distinguish them. Only the cobnut is grown in North America. The main exporters of hazelnuts are Mediterranean countries, with Turkey being the largest producer in the world and Germany and England ranking first and second, respectively, in consumption. They are rich in some of the B vitamins as well as C and E, and they are a good source of protein. They will keep for many months in a cool place and up to two years in the refrigerator.

MACADAMIAS

Macadamias are also called Queensland nuts, because they originated in the forests of Queensland in northeastern Australia. Many Australian macadamia trees are 100 to 150 years old. They are the only indigenous Australian plant ever developed into a cash crop. They are cultivated on a large scale, however, only in Hawaii, where they have thrived in the rich volcanic soil since being introduced in 1882. Macadamias were supposedly named by Australia's foremost botanist, Baron Ferdinand Van Mueller, in 1857, for his friend Dr John MacAdam, who never saw or ate one. Macadamias are harvested when they fall from their trees. Given their hard shells and tendency to mildew in the shell, they are almost always sold shelled – raw or roasted. Because their high oil content makes them spoil rapidly they are usually sold in vacuum-packed jars. Once the container is opened, the nuts should be consumed quickly, which is usually not a problem.

PEANUTS

Not really a nut, but rather a legume or pea, the peanut originated in South America, in the tropical lower Andes of Bolivia. Today peanuts are grown in every subtropical region on earth, thanks to the intervention of humans. The world's largest growers are China and India, but their production is consumed domestically mostly in the form of oil. Nigeria, where the Portuguese introduced the nut, is todays largest exporter. The two types of peanut, Spanish and Virginia, both grow underground, encased in fibrous shells. (Peanuts have also been known as groundnuts or monkeynuts.) Virginia peanuts are a bit longer and have a stronger taste but are otherwise indistinguishable from Spanish.

Both varieties are highly nutritious, with approximately 25 per cent protein as well as some of the B vitamins, vitamin E and minerals such as phosphorus and iron. Peanuts are also high in unsaturated fat, and peanut oil's high smoking point permits frying at high temperatures without burning. Unshelled, peanuts will keep for several months in a cool, dry place. Shelled, they will keep for two months in a cool place – longer in the refrigerator.

PECANS

This former staple food of the indigenous peoples of North America is the only truly "All-American" nut. A species of hickory, the pecan grows wild on tall trees in the temperate zones. Wild pecans tend to be smaller than cultivated ones and have a lower percentage of kernel and more shell. Pecans are harvested by shaking the trees, causing the nuts to fall to the ground. They are slightly less fatty than their relative the walnut, but their 70 per cent oil content – 95 per cent of it unsaturated – causes them to turn rancid soon after shelling.

Pecans are rich in several useful minerals and some B vitamins, and they are an excellent source of B6, which is present almost exclusively in foods that require cooking, which destroys this vitamin. Unshelled pecans will keep in a cool place for a few months. Shelled pecans, stored in an airtight container, will last for a few weeks in the refrigerator.

PINE NUTS

Also known as pine kernels, pignolias and Indian nuts, the nuts of many pine trees are edible and have been used in cuisines the world over for centuries. Only the nuts of the stone pine, however, which grows wild from Portugal to the Black Sea, are cultivated globally as a cash crop. Pine nuts have a soft shell and no skin, and all commercially available types are sold shelled. Some varieties, such as the pinon of the southwestern United States, are available only locally. Although expensive, pine nuts have a strong resinous flavour that allows cooks to use fewer of them than other milder nuts. This flavour mellows when the nuts are roasted. Pine nuts spoil quickly and should always be refrigerated in an airtight container where they will last for a few weeks.

PISTACHIOS

Pistachios are native to central and western Asia and were brought to Rome from Syria in the first century. The Mongol emperors referred to pistachios as the nuts of paradise, but their new European admirers called them green almonds. Today the pistachio tree, a six-metre-tall deciduous species of turpentine tree, thrives in the poor rocky soil of the Mediterranean, the Middle East and the southwestern USA. The nuts are encased in a gummy husk, which is removed by soaking. As the nuts dry the shells gape open and take on their familiar appearance. Pistachio shells are naturally tan; red pistachios have been dyed and should be avoided.

WALNUTS

Walnuts are native to the temperate zones of Europe and Asia and were introduced long ago to similar climates all over the world. Their well-preserved remains have even been found in Pompeii. Walnut trees have long been considered an excellent source of timber, and walnuts were once believed to ward off disease and increase fertility (inspiring the custom of scattering them at weddings in some cultures the way others use rice). Walnuts come in two varieties: the European, also called the English or Persian; and the black. The European variety of which France is the leading producer became known as English walnuts because the English had a thriving trade in them in centuries past. But as with almonds, Spanish missionaries introduced them to North America via California. Because black walnuts are hard to crack, with sticky shells, they have resisted commercial exploitation. Some consider them less tasty than European walnuts, but this has not prevented their use in desserts and ice cream. The husks and casings of European walnuts are used to make a liqueur known in Europe as brou. Walnuts have a high fat content, most of it unsaturated, and they should be kept refrigerated in an airtight container once shelled.

SHELLING, PEELING, TOASTING AND ROASTING

ALMONDS

To shell: Cover with boiling water and soak for 15 to 20 minutes. Drain and cool. Crack with a nutcracker.

To peel (or blanch): Drop into boiling water, boil for 1 minute, then drain and rinse in cold water. Pinch one end of the skin, and the nut will pop out the other end. Watch out for flying almonds!

To toast: Heat 1 tablespoon butter or oil for each cup of nuts in a skillet large enough to hold the nuts in one layer. Sauté over medium-low heat, tossing frequently to prevent burning, until golden brown, 15·to 30 minutes. Almonds can also be deep-fried.

To roast: Preheat the oven to 180ºC (350ºF or gas mark 4). Place the almonds in a single layer in a shallow pan and roast, stirring often, until golden brown, about 30 to 45 minutes. The almonds will continue to cook after being removed from the oven, so be sure to take them out just before the desired degree of doneness.

BRAZIL NUTS

To shell: Drop into boiling water and boil gently for 3 minutes, Drain and cool. Crack with a nutcracker or preheat the oven to 200ºC (400ºF or gas mark 7) and roast in the shell in a shallow pan in a single layer for about 20 minutes. Then cool, crack and shell.
To peel: Drop into boiling water with 1$\frac{1}{2}$ teaspoons baking soda for each quart of water. Simmer for 2 minutes, slip off the skins while the nuts are still warm. To toast: Heat 1 tablespoon butter or oil per cup of nuts in a skillet large enough to hold the nuts in one layer. Sauté over medium heat for 5 to 10 minutes for whole nuts or 2 to 3 minutes for sliced nuts, stirring often, until golden brown.

To roast: Follow the instructions for roasting almonds, but decrease the time to 20 to 30 minutes, or roast in the shell as previously described.

To slice: Cover with cold water in a saucepan. Bring slowly to a boil, lower the heat and simmer for 2 to 3 minutes. This makes it possible to slice the nuts without breaking them.

CASHEWS

Cashews are always sold shelled and peeled.

To toast: Follow the instructions for toasting almonds.

To roast: Follow the instructions for roasting almonds, but decrease the roasting time to 10 to 20 minutes.

To shell and peal: Preheat the oven to 200ºC (400ºF or gas mark 7). Cut an X on the flat side of each chestnut. Roast in a shallow pan in a single layer for about 20 minutes or until the chestnuts feel soft. Shell and peel the chestnuts as soon as they are cool enough to handle. (Expect to burn your fingers slightly). Use a sharp knife to get the shelling started. Pull off the shell and as much of the skin as possible. Chestnuts with stubborn skins can be reheated, either in water or in the oven, or even in oil in a skillet. Try peeling again, gently squeezing the chestnut or even breaking it apart if necessary.

You can also "cheat" and buy the imported French brands of chestnuts that come vacuum-packed or packed in water. They are delicious and can save you a lot of time.

HAZELNUTS

To shell: Crack with a nutcracker. To roast and peel: Preheat the oven to 180ºC (350ºF or gas mark 4). Spread the nuts in a single layer on a baking tray or in a shallow tin. Dry the nuts in the oven for about 15 minutes or until the skins begin to flake and the nuts appear light brown. Remove from the oven and wrap in a piece of kitchen paper. Place the kitchen paper in a plastic bag until the nuts are cool enough to handle. Rub the hazelnuts together in the kitchen paper rubbing off as much of the brown skin as possible. The hazelnuts are now roasted and peeled. Alternatively put them under the grill for a few minutes until the skins flake. Then proceed as directed.

MACADAMIAS

Virtually all macadamia nuts are sold shelled. Some are already roasted and salted, so be sure to check the label.

To roast: Follow the instructions for roasting almonds, but reduce the time to 12 to 15 minutes.

PEANUTS

To shell and peel: You can usually shell and peel peanuts by hand, either before or after roasting. If removing the brown skins proves difficult, cover the shelled peanuts with boiling water and set aside for 5 minutes. Drain. The skins should then slide off quite easily but the nuts must then dry for several hours or for several minutes in the oven.

To roast: Follow the instructions for roasting almonds. Shelled peanuts should roast to a nice golden brown in 15 to 20 minutes. In the shell, roast them for about 25 minutes.

To toast: Peanuts are usually toasted by deep frying but may be toasted as almonds, reducing the time to 8 to 10 minutes. To deep-fry: heat enough oil to cover the peanuts to 180°C (350°F or gas mark 4). As when roasting, these nuts will continue to cook after being removed from the oil, so stop toasting just before they are done to your satisfaction.

COCONUTS

One coconut weighing approximately 1½ pounds yields about 4 cups flesh.

To shell and peel: Preheat the oven to 200°C (400°F or gas mark 7). Poke holes in the 3 coconut eyes with an ice pick or other sharp object. Drain the liquid (this is not coconut milk) and taste a few drops. If it tastes at all sour, discard the coconut and try another one. Discard the liquid unless the flesh is to be frozen. Place the coconut in the oven for 20 minutes, then let it cool slightly. Holding it over a large howl, strike it all the way around the centre with the back edge of a large, heavy knife or cleaver until it splits. Pry the heavy shell off with a screwdriver and remove the thin brown skin with a vegetable peeler. Wash and dry the coconut flesh, then grate or shred according to the recipe.

To save time with little loss of taste, buy frozen grated unsweetened coconut - available in ethnic markets or specialist shops. To freeze your own coconut either in chunks or grated, strain the reserved liquid from the center and combine it with the flesh in an airtight container. To toast: Preheat the oven to 180°C (350°F or gas mark 4). Spread freshly grated or shredded coconut in a shallow pan and toast for 5 to 10 minutes, or until golden

brown. Stir occasionally to toast evenly. Cool on paper towels. For faster but less even toasting, spread in a shallow pan and place 3 to 4 inches under the grill for 3 to 6 minutes, or until golden brown. Stir often and watch carefully to make sure it does not burn.
To make coconut milk from fresh coconut: Shell and peel the coconut as directed. When all of the flesh is washed and dried, cut it into 1-inch or smaller squares and put half of them into the bowl of a blender or food processor fitted with a steel blade. Bring 3 cups water or milk - or a combination - almost to a boil. Pour half of it into the blender with the coconut flesh and process as finely as possible. Line a bowl with a double thickness of cheesecloth and pour the processed mixture into it. Repeat with the second half of the flesh and liquid. Pick up the edges of the cheesecloth and raise it slowly allowing the liquid to drain out. Squeeze the cheesecloth gently to extract the remaining liquid but not the pulp. This should yield about 3 cups. Seal in an airtight container. The milk will keep for 2 to 3 days in the refrigerator or several months in the freezer.

Dried coconut, which will keep indefinitely in an airtight container, works well when preparing coconut milk. Proceed as for fresh coconut, using 3 to 4 cups dried coconut and an equal amount of liquid. Good canned coconut milks are available at Asian and specialist markets. If you buy sweetened coconut milk, you will have to compensate accordingly in the recipes.

ONE
APPETISERS
AND SOUPS

CHICKEN LIVER AND PISTACHIO PATÉ

90 g (3 oz) unsalted butter

450 g (1 lb) chicken livers, washed and drained

75 g (2½ oz) chopped celery ribs and tops from the celery heart

150 g (5 oz) chopped mushrooms

90 g (3 oz) chopped onion

1 garlic clove, chopped

4 tablespoons cognac or brandy

¼ teaspoon cayenne pepper

2 teaspoons dry mustard

¼ teaspoon freshly grated nutmeg

¼ teaspoon dried thyme, crushed

¼ teaspoon ground allspice

½ teaspoon salt

½ teaspoon freshly ground black pepper

150 g (5 oz) shelled, peeled, dried and roasted pistachios

Serves 12 to 16.

Preparation time: 30 minutes,

plus 4 hours to set and 30 minutes to come to room temperature.

Preheat the oven to 150ºC (300ºF or gas 1-2).

In a large frying pan over medium-high heat, melt 60 g (2 oz) of the butter and add the chicken livers, celery, mushrooms, onion and garlic. Cook for 3 to 5 minutes or until the livers have begun to brown lightly but are still pink inside. Add the cognac or brandy, cover, lower the heat and simmer for 5 more minutes. Remove from the heat and place the contents in the bowl of a blender or food processor fitted with a steel blade. Add the spices and the remaining butter cut into chunks, and process until smooth. (While processing the mixture, stop several times to scrape down the sides of the bowl.)

Fold the nuts, reserving a few for garnish, into the processed liver mixture by hand. Pour the mixture into a 750-ml to 1 litre (2-pint) crock, bowl, mould or terrine and refrigerate for 4 hours or overnight, until firm.

Serve in the crock or bowl or unmould onto a plate by dipping the container into hot water for a few moments, covering it with the plate and inverting. Garnish with the reserved pistachios, whole or chopped.

Allow the pate to stand at room temperature for 30 minutes before serving.

COLD NOODLES WITH SPICY ALMOND SAUCE

4 tablespoons vegetable oil

120 g (4 oz) slivered blanched almonds

2 tablespoons soy sauce

3 tablespoons white rice vinegar (white wine vinegar may be substituted)

1 teaspoon sugar1 tablespoon grated fresh ginger

2 garlic cloves, crushed

2 tablespoons dry sherry

2-3 tablespoons hot chilli oil (to taste)

450 g (1 lb) soba noodles or spaghetti

3 shallots, thinly sliced diagonally

1 18-cm (7-inch) cucumber peeled, seeded and cut into matchsticks

In a 25-cm (10-inch) skillet over medium-high heat, heat 3 tablespoons of the vegetable oil. Add the almonds and fry until brown, about 2 minutes. Remove about ½ of the almonds with a slotted spoon and drain them on a piece of kitchen paper. Reserve.

Put the remaining almonds and the oil into the bowl of a blender or food processor fitted with a steel blade. Process, pulsing on and off, until a smooth "butter" forms.

Add the next 7 ingredients to the food processor and continue to process until the mixture is smooth and well combined. (The mixture may be made up to several days in advance to this point, refrigerated and brought to room temperature before serving.)

Cook the noodles until *al dente* according to package directions. Drain and rinse under cold water until they are thoroughly cooled. Drain again. Toss the noodles with the remaining tablespoon of oil and serve on a platter or individual plates, topped with the sauce and garnished with the shallots, cucumber and reserved almonds.

Serves 4.

Preparation time: 40 minutes

FRESH FIGS WITH BLACK PEPPER AND HAZELNUTS

120 g (4 oz) shelled, roasted and peeled hazelnuts

1 tablespoon hazelnut oil (vegetable oil may be substituted)

8 ripe fresh figs

2 teaspoons freshly cracked black pepper

Place the hazelnuts in the bowl of a blender or food processor fitted with a steel blade. Grind the nuts, pulsing on and off a couple of times, until the ground nuts begin to stick together. Add the oil and continue to grind until a crunchy nut butter has formed.

Cut the figs in half lengthways. Place a dollop of approximately $1/2$ tablespoon nut butter in the cavity of each half and sprinkle with $1/4$ teaspoon pepper.

Serve on individual appetiser plates or on a single large plate as part of an hors d'oeuvre table.

Serves 4.

Preparation time: 10 minutes.

CHEDDAR, BEER AND PECAN CHEESECAKE

45 g (1½ oz) unsalted butter

380 g (13 oz) roasted pecan pieces or halves

90 g (3 oz) unbleached plain flour

½ teaspoon freshly ground white pepper

½ teaspoon cayenne pepper

1 teaspoon dry mustard

2 teaspoons Worcestershire sauce

150 ml (¼ pint) beer or ale

450 g (1 lb) sharp cheddar cheese, finely shredded

450 g (1 lb) cream cheese at room temperature

4 large eggs at room temperature

Serves 16 as an appetiser, 8 as a mainmeal.

Preparation time: 2 hours, plus overnight to chill and 2 to 3 hours to come to room temperature.

Preheat the oven to 180ºC (350ºF or gas 4).

Melt the butter and set it aside.

Generously grease a 20-cm (8-inch) springform cake tin. Set the tin in the centre of a 30-cm (12-inch) square of aluminium foil and fold the foil up the sides of the tin, pressing it firmly against them.

In a blender or food processor fitted with a steel blade, process 230 g (8 oz) of the roasted pecans with 45 g (1½ oz) of the flour pulsing on and off, until the mixture resembles bread crumbs. Place the mixture in a small bowl and add the melted butter mixing well. Firmly press the mixture into the bottom and halfway up the sides of the springform cake tin. Put the tin in the oven and bake for 10 minutes. Remove and cool to room temperature.

While the crust is baking, coarsely chop the remaining nuts and set aside. Then combine the white pepper, cayenne pepper, dry mustard and Worcestershire sauce in a 1-litre (1¾ -pint) saucepan and whisk to remove any lumps. Add the beer or ale and whisk to combine. Heat over medium heat until the beer is hot and steaming. Remove from the heat.

Add the cheddar cheese and whisk until smooth. (The mixture will look somewhat grainy. It should be only slightly warm to the touch. If not, let it cool slightly).

In a large mixing bowl, beat the cream cheese until fluffy. Beat in the cheddar mixture and the remaining 45 g (1½ oz) flour until combined. Add the eggs one at a time, blending well after each addition. Fold in the remaining nuts.

Pour the mixture into the cooled crust. Bake for 40 minutes. Turn off the heat and let the cheesecake sit undisturbed in the oven for an additional 40 minutes.

Remove the cake from the oven, cool completely then refrigerate overnight.

Remove the cake from the refrigerator a few hours before serving and allow to come to room temperature. Carefully remove the cake from the tin. Slice and serve with tangy pickles and pickled onions if desired, or place on an hors d'oeuvre table.

FRIED WALNUT POLENTA WITH GORGONZOLA SAUCE

Polenta: 60 g (2 oz) unsalted butter

750 ml (1¼ pints) milk

1/2 teaspoon salt

120 g (4 oz) stone-ground yellow cornmeal

150 g (5 oz) chopped walnuts

Sauce:

375 ml (12 fl oz) milk

30 g (1 oz) unsalted butter

15 g (½ oz) minced spring onion

45 g (1½ oz) unbleached plain flour

60 g (2 oz) crumbled Gorgonzola cheese

salt and freshly ground black pepper to taste

parsley leaves for garnish (optional)

Serves 8.

Preparation time: 1 hour plus 2 hours or overnight to chill.

Make the polenta. (This can be done a day ahead or earlier in the day) Butter a

21-x 11-cm (8½- x 4½-inch) loaf tin or a 1.5-litre (2½-pint) mould with 15 g (½ oz) of the butter.

In a heavy saucepan over medium-high heat, combine the milk, salt, and another 15 g (½ oz) of the butter. Heat to a simmer. While whisking constantly add the cornmeal in a trickle. When all the cornmeal has been added, lower the heat, maintaining a simmer and cook, stirring constantly with a wooden spoon, until the mixture is thick enough to pull away from the sides of the tin, about 25 to 30 minutes. Stir in the chopped walnuts until well distributed. Pour immediately into the prepared tin. Cool, then cover and refrigerate for at least 2 hours or overnight.

Unmould the polenta by inverting the tin onto a board or plate and rubbing the pan with a towel dipped in hot water and wrung out. With a sharp knife, slice the unmoulded polenta into 1-cm (½-inch) thick slices.

To make the sauce, scald the milk in a small saucepan. (Heat it until bubbles form around the edge of the pan.) Remove from the heat.

In another small saucepan, melt 30 g (1 oz) of butter over medium-high heat, add the spring onion and sauté until it begins to look translucent, about 3 to 4 minutes. Add the flour and whisk constantly until bubbling but not browned, another 2 to 3 minutes. Whisk in the milk, stirring until smooth. Add the cheese and the salt and pepper to taste. Whisk until smooth. Lower the heat to low and simmer until thick, about 10 minutes.

Meanwhile, in a large frying pan, melt the remaining 30 g (1 oz) of butter over medium-high heat and sauté the polenta slices in batches, turning them over once, until golden brown on both sides. Serve hot, 2 slices per serving, with the sauce as well as parsley leaves for garnish if desired.

GINGERED CHESTNUT SOUP

30 g (1 oz) unsalted butter 1 large onion, chopped

2.5 g (8 oz) carrots, scraped and chopped (about 3 or 4 carrots)

45 g (1½ oz) chopped fresh ginger

450 g (1 lb) chestnuts, roasted, shelled and peeled

1 bay leaf

salt and freshly ground white pepper to taste

1 litre (1¾ pints) chicken stock

250 ml (8 fl oz) dry white wine

40 ml (1½ fl oz) fresh lemon juice

sour cream for garnish

Serves 6.

Preparation time: 1 hour 15 minutes.

Melt the butter in a large saucepan over medium heat. Add the onion, carrots and ginger and sauté gently for 10 minutes.

Add the chestnuts, bay leaf, salt and white pepper and broth. Bring the mixture to a boil, then cover lower the heat and simmer for 45 minutes. Remove the bay leaf. Purée the mixture in batches in a blender or food processor fitted with a steel blade. Add the wine and lemon juice. (The soup can be prepared in advance to this point and refrigerated.)

Rinse the saucepan thoroughly return the puréed soup to it and heat slowly stirring frequently to prevent sticking. You may add more stock if the soup is too thick for your taste, but remember that it will thin a little as it heats.

Serve garnished with a dollop of sour cream.

COCONUT-PRAWN SOUP

1 litre (2 pints) coconut milk, made from 2 fresh coconuts (canned unsweetened coconut milk may be substituted)

2 medium-size onions, chopped

1 garlic clove, crushed

10 black peppercorns

3 coriander seeds

zest of 1 lemon, removed with a vegetable peeler or sharp knife

1 teaspoon cumin seeds

3 parsley sprigs

1 or 2 hot fresh chillies (to taste), seeded and coarsely chopped

450 g (1 lb) raw prawns, shelled, deveined and chopped

1 teaspoon sugar

40 ml (1½ fl oz) fresh lemon juice salt to taste

4-6 peeled cooked prawns for garnish (optional)

15 g ½ oz) shredded fresh coconut for garnish (optional)

Serves 4 to 6.

Preparation time: 2 hours.

Place the coconut milk and onions in a medium-size saucepan and bring to a boil. Place the garlic, peppercorns, coriander seeds, lemon zest, cumin seeds, parsley and chillies in a spice bag or a piece of cheesecloth, tied shut, and add it to the saucepan. Cover, lower the heat and simmer for 25 minutes.

Add the prawns, sugar, lemon juice and salt to taste and simmer for 5 minutes more. Remove the spice bag. Serve hot, garnished with whole prawns and shredded coconut if desired.

CRANBERRY-ALMOND SOUP

150 g (5 oz) blanched almonds

175 g (6 oz) granulated sugar

875 ml (1½ pints) water

1 8-cm (3-inch) cinnamon stick

440 g (15 oz) cranberries

250 ml (8 fl oz) rosé wine

Serves 6 to 8.

Preparation time: 30 minutes.

Place the almonds and half the sugar in a blender or food processor fitted with a steel blade. Grind the mixture to a paste. Add 125 ml (4 fl oz) of the water and process again until the paste is very smooth. Set aside.

In a medium-size saucepan, bring the remaining 750 ml (1¼ pints) water to a boil. Add the remaining sugar and the cinnamon stick and stir to dissolve the sugar. Add the cranberries and the almond paste and return to a boil, mashing some of the berries against the side of the saucepan. Cover, reduce the heat and simmer for 15 minutes. Add the wine and simmer for 5 minutes more. Remove the cinnamon stick and serve.

BORSCHT WITH HAZELNUT CREAM

4 medium-size beets
(about 900 g [2 lbs])

15 g (^{1}/$_2$ oz) unsalted butter

1 small onion, chopped

60 g (2 oz) chopped carrot

1 small garlic clove, chopped

1 teaspoon granulated sugar

^{1}/$_4$ teaspoon ground cloves

750 ml (1^1/$_4$ pints) chicken stock

1 tablespoon fresh lemon juice

salt and freshly ground white pepper to taste

120 g (4 oz) shelled, roasted and peeled hazelnuts (page 13)

150 g (5 oz) sour cream

snipped fresh chives for garnish

Serves 6.

Preparation time: 1 hour 15 minutes, plus several hours or overnight to chill.

Trim the beetroots, leaving the roots and 2 inches of the stems attached. Scrub them well, put them in a large pot and cover them with cold water. Bring the water to a boil, cover, lower the heat and simmer for 25 to 30 minutes, until the beetroots are tender. Drop the beets into cold water and let sit until they are cool enough to handle. Peel and cut them into 1-cm (^{1}/$_2$-inch) cubes. Set aside. In a 3-litre (5^1/$_2$-pint) saucepan, melt the butter over medium heat. Sauté the onion and carrot for about 7 minutes, until the onion is soft and translucent. Add the garlic, sugar cloves, reserved beetroots and stock. Bring to a boil, cover lower the heat and simmer for about 20 minutes.

Purée half the cooked mixture in a blender or food processor fitted with a steel blade. Pour it into a bowl or container and then process the remaining soup. Add lemon juice and salt and pepper to taste.

Cover and cool the puréed soup. Refrigerate it for several hours or overnight. Shortly before serving, place the hazelnuts in a blender or food processor fitted with a steel blade and process until they are puréed, stopping occasionally to scrape the sides. Add the sour cream and process until just combined. Refrigerate until serving time.

Serve the soup cold in bowls topped with a dollop of hazelnut cream and some snipped chives.

TWO
BREADS AND
SIDE DISHES

PEANUT BUTTER BISCUITS

150 g (5 oz) unbleached plain flour

1 tablespoon baking powder

$^1/_2$ teaspoon baking soda

$^1/_2$ teaspoon salt

90 g (3 oz) whole wheat flour

205 g (7 oz) crunchy peanut butter (made without sugar or salt)

175 ml (6 fl oz) buttermilk

1 tablespoon honey

Makes 8 or 9 biscuits.
Preparation time: 30 minutes.

Preheat the oven to 230°C (450°F or gas 8). Grease a 23-cm (9-inch) round cake tin.

Sift together the plain flour, baking powder, baking soda and salt. Add the whole wheat flour and stir to blend.

With a pastry blender, your fingers, or 2 knives, cut the peanut butter into the dry ingredients until they are thoroughly dispersed.

Combine the buttermilk and honey, add the mixture to the dough, and stir until combined.

Turn the dough onto a floured board or work top and knead for 30 seconds. Roll or pat out to a 2.5-cm (1-inch) thickness. Cut the dough with a 6-cm (2$^1/_2$-inch) biscuit cutter or an inverted floured drinking glass.

Place the biscuits, evenly spaced, in the prepared tin and bake for 12 to 15 minutes, until golden brown. Serve hot.

DATE AND PISTACHIO SCONES

300 g (10 oz) unbleached plain flour

60 g (2 oz) firmly packed soft dark brown sugar

2$^1/_2$ teaspoons baking powder

$^1/_2$ teaspoon baking soda

$^1/_2$ teaspoon salt

$^1/_4$ teaspoon ground cinnamon

grated zest of 1 lemon

60 g (2 oz) unsalted butter frozen (cold if you are not using a food processor)

175 ml (6 fl oz) buttermilk

1$^1/_2$ teaspoons vanilla essence

225 g (8 oz) pitted dates, chopped

150 g (5 oz) shelled and peeled pistachios

1 large egg yolk

$^1/_2$ teaspoon water

Makes 8 scones.
Preparation time: 45 minutes.

Preheat the oven to 200°C (400°F or gas 6-7). Grease a baking tray or large pizza tin.

In a food processor fitted with a steel blade (or in a large bowl if you are making the dough by hand), place the flour, brown sugar, baking powder, baking soda, salt, cinnamon and lemon zest. Pulse for 1 to 2 seconds or stir together. If processing, cut the frozen butter into 8 pieces and add it to the bowl. Process, pulsing on and off, just until the mixture resembles coarse meal. Do not over-process. (By hand, cut the cold butter into 1-cm ($^1/_2$-inch) cubes and work into the flour mixture with a pastry blender, 2 knives or your fingers until it resembles coarse meal.)

Combine the buttermilk and vanilla essence. With the motor running, add the liquid all at once to the food processor and process just until the mixture forms a ball. (By hand, stir in the liquids and mix until thoroughly combined.) Turn the dough out onto a floured board. Mix in the dates and all but 60 g (2oz) of the nuts by hand until well distributed.

On a floured board, pat or roll out the dough to a 2-cm ($^3/_4$-inch) thickness. Cut it into 7.5-cm (3-inch) triangles with a sharp knife. Place 2.5 cm (1 inch) apart in the prepared tin.

Beat the egg yolk with the water and brush it over the top of each scone. Chop the reserved nuts and sprinkle over the top.

Bake for 15 to 20 minutes, until lightly browned and a skewer inserted in the middle comes out clean. Cool for 5 minutes. Serve immediately cutting the scones apart if necessary or separate and cool completely on a wire rack. Store in an airtight container.

BLUEBERRY AND ALMOND MUFFINS

150 g (5 oz) unbleached plain flour

2 teaspoons baking powder

$^1\!/_2$ teaspoon ground cinnamon

$^1\!/_2$ teaspoon salt

120 g (4 oz) granulated sugar

1 large egg

60 g (2 oz) unsalted butter melted

150 ml (5 fl oz) milk

1 teaspoon grated lemon zest

$^1\!/_2$ teaspoon almond essence

150 g (5 oz) fresh or unthawed blueberries

150 g (5 oz) shelled, toasted and coarsely chopped almonds

Makes 6 muffins.

Preparation time: 40 minutes.

Preheat the oven to 200ºC (400ºF or gas 6-7). Grease and flour 6 7.5-cm (3-inch) muffin cups (deep bun tins).

Sift the flour, baking powder, cinnamon and salt together into a large mixing bowl.

In another bowl, whisk together the sugar and egg until the mixture is pale and lemon-coloured. Whisk in the melted butter and milk and then the lemon zest and almond essence.

Gently stir the liquid mixture into the dry mixture, stirring just until the dry ingredients are thoroughly moistened but still lumpy. Fold in the berries and nuts just until they are evenly distributed. Do not overmix.

Fill the muffin cups (deep bun tins) to the top and bake for 20 to 25 minutes or until the muffins are golden brown and spring back when pressed lightly. Cool, at least slightly in the tin or on wire racks. Serve while still warm or at room temperature. The muffins may be stored in an airtight container and reheated if desired.

HAZELNUT AND HONEY MUFFINS

175 g (6 oz) unbleached plain flour

1 tablespoon baking powder

205 g (7 oz) rolled oats

$^1\!/_2$ teaspoon baking soda

$^1\!/_2$ teaspoon salt

175 g (6 oz) plain yoghurt

150 g (5 oz) honey

$1^1\!/_2$ teaspoons vanilla essence

1 large egg

4 tablespoons hazelnut oil (vegetable oil may be substituted)

225 g (8 oz) coarsely chopped roasted hazelnuts

Makes 1 dozen muffins.

Preparation time: 45 minutes.

Preheat the oven to 230ºC (450ºF or gas 8). Grease a dozen 6-cm (2$^1\!/_2$-inch) muffin cups.

In a large mixing bowl, combine the flour, baking powder, oats, baking soda and salt. Mix well.

In another bowl, whisk together the yoghurt, honey, vanilla essence, egg and oil.

Combine the dry and wet ingredients, stirring just until the dry ingredients are thoroughly moistened. Fold in the toasted hazelnuts just until they are well distributed. Do not overmix. The batter should be lumpy.

Heap the mixture into the muffin cups (deep bun tins) so it is about 1 cm ($^1\!/_2$ inch) above the top of the tin and evenly distributed. Bake for 18 to 20 minutes or until the muffins are golden brown and spring back when pressed lightly

Remove from the tin and cool on a wire rack for at least 5 minutes. Serve warm or cool. Store in an airtight container. The muffins may be reheated if desired.

PECAN AND PROSCIUTTO BREAD

175 g (6 oz) prosciutto, chopped

75 g (2½ oz) unsalted butter margarine or vegetable shortening at room temperature

300 ml (10 fl oz) warm water (40-44°C [105-115°F])

7 g (¼ oz) envelope active dry yeast

2 teaspoons granulated sugar

500-560 g (18-19 oz) bread flour (unbleached plain flour may be substituted, with some loss in rising)

1½ teaspoons freshly cracked black pepper

225 g (8 oz) coarsely chopped pecans

2 teaspoons cornmeal

Makes 1 baguette.

Preparation time: 3 hours.

Grease the inside of a large bowl. Set aside.

Sauté the prosciutto in a frying pan in 15 g (½ oz) of the butter over medium heat for about 2 minutes. Pour the meat and butter into a large ungreased mixing bowl. Add the warm water, yeast and sugar to the bowl. Stir to combine. Mix in 120 (4 oz) of the flour and 60 g (2 oz) of the remaining butter. Stir until well combined. Add the pepper, pecans and 350 g (12 oz) of the remaining flour. Mix well.

Spread 60 g (2 oz) flour on your work surface and turn the dough out onto it. Knead, incorporating more flour as needed to keep the dough from sticking. Do not use any more flour than necessary. Knead for about 5 minutes, until the dough is smooth and elastic.

Form the dough into a ball and place it in the greased bowl. Turn the dough over so it is greased on all sides, cover the bowl and let the dough rise in a warm place until doubled in size, about 1 hour to 1 hour 30 minutes.

Sprinkle the cornmeal over a baking tray or baguette tin. Set aside.

Melt the remaining 15 g (½ oz) of butter and set aside.

When the dough has doubled, knock it down with your fist and turn it out onto a lightly floured surface. Roll or pat the dough into a 25- x 32-cm (10- x 15-inch) rectangle. Roll the dough up tightly Swiss-roll fashion. Pinch the ends and the edges of the dough to seal it. Place it on the prepared tin, seam down, with the ends tucked under it. Brush it with the melted butter. Cover it loosely with plastic wrap and let it rise in a warm place until it has again doubled in size, about 30 minutes. About halfway through the second rise, preheat the oven to 190°C (375°F or gas 5). Bake the bread for about 30 minutes, until it is browned and sounds hollow when tapped. Cool on a wire rack.

CURRIED CORN AND COCONUT TIMBALES

225 g (8 oz) fresh corn kernels, cut or grated from the cob (about 6 ears)

3 large eggs

45 g (1½ oz) fresh crustless white bread crumbs

30 g (1 oz) grated onion

30 g (1 oz) freshly grated coconut

125 ml (4 fl oz) coconut milk

½ teaspoon salt

1 teaspoon good-quality curry powder

¼ teaspoon freshly ground white pepper

30 g (1 oz) shredded and toasted unsweetened coconut for garnish (optional)

Serves 6.

Preparation time: 50 minutes.

Preheat the oven to 180°C (350°F or gas 4). Butter 6 175-g (6-oz) ramekins and set aside.

In a mixing bowl, combine all the ingredients except the toasted coconut. Mix thoroughly Pour the mixture into the prepared ramekins, filling them about ¾ full.

Place the ramekins in a roasting tin and pour enough water into the pan to reach halfway up the sides of the cups.

Bake the timbales for 5 minutes, then lower the oven temperature to 160°C (325°F or gas 3) and continue to bake for 25 to 30 minutes, until the timbales are set and a toothpick inserted in the centre comes out clean.

Cool the timbales in the cups for 10 minutes. Then serve, either in the cups or inverted and unmoulded onto plates. Top with toasted coconut if desired.

BRAISED CHESTNUTS WITH ONIONS AND PRUNES

30 g (1 oz) bacon grease or unsalted butter

450 g (1 lb) chestnuts, shelled and peeled

450 g (1 lb) small white onions, peeled

500 ml (1 pint) beef stock

250 ml (8 fl oz) good-quality port wine

45 g (1½ oz) firmly packed soft dark brown sugar

1 bay leaf 225 g (8 oz) pitted prunes

salt and freshly ground black pepper to taste

In a large, heavy sauté pan, melt 2 tablespoons of the grease or butter over medium heat and sauté the chestnuts until lightly browned, about 7 minutes. Remove with a slotted spoon and reserve.

Add another tablespoon of the grease or butter and sauté the onions until lightly browned, about 5 to 7 minutes. Return the chestnuts to the pan and add the stock, port, brown sugar and bay leaf. Bring to a boil, then lower the heat and simmer for 30 minutes, stirring gently several times. Add the prunes and return to a simmer. Continue to simmer, stirring gently several times, for 30 to 35 minutes more or until the liquid has formed a syrupy glaze.

Remove the bay leaf, season to taste with salt and pepper and serve hot. This recipe may be made a day in advance and reheated by adding 125 ml (4 fl oz) more stock and cooking on low heat until the syrupy glaze has re-formed.

Serves 6.

Preparation time: 1 hour 20 minutes.

VIDALIA ONIONS STUFFED WITH APPLES AND CASHEWS

6 well-formed large fresh Vidalia or other sweet onions (about 7.5 cm [3 inches] in diameter)

salt and freshly ground black pepper to taste

90 g (3 oz) unsalted butter at room temperature

2 medium-size tart apples, such as Granny Smith

90 g (3 oz) chopped roasted cashews

15 g (1/2 oz) finely chopped parsley

1 1/2 teaspoons finely chopped fresh tarragon (or 1/2 teaspoon dried)

250-375 ml (8-12 fl oz) dry white wine

Serves 6.

Preparation time: 1 hour 45 minutes.

Preheat the oven to 180°C (350°F or gas mark 4).

Trim the root end of each onion slightly to make a flat base. Slice off the other end leaving a cut surface 5 to 6 cm (2 to 2 1/2 inches) in diameter. Peel each onion and dig out the flesh with a melon baller, leaving the bottoms and sides about 1 cm (1/2 inch) thick. Chop 350 g (12 oz) of the onion flesh, and salt and pepper the inside of the onions.

In a frying pant, melt 4 tablespoons of butter over medium heat. Sauté the chopped onion for about 5 minutes, stirring frequently Peel, core and chop apples and add them to the pan. Sauté for about 10 minutes more, until just beginning to brown. Remove from the heat.

Stir in all but 2 tablespoons of the cashews to the onion and apple mixture, then the parsley and tarragon.

Melt 1 tablespoon of the remaining butter.

With the remaining tablespoon of butter, butter the outsides of the cored onions and the inside of a pan just large enough to hold them. Pack the onions with the stuffing (don't press too hard), and place them in the prepared pan. Top with the reserved cashews and drizzle with the melted butter.

Bring the wine to a boil in a small saucepan and pour it 2 to 2.5 cm (3/4 to 1 inch) deep around the onions. Place the pan in the lower part of your oven. Bake for about 1 hour, basting frequently or until the onions are tender.

TOMATOES STUFFED WITH SAFFRON RICE AND BRAZIL NUTS

6 large ripe but firm tomatoes (approximately 7.5 cm [3 inches] in diameter)

1 teaspoon salt

375 ml (12 fl oz) chicken stock

1/2 teaspoon saffron threads, crushed

2 tablespoons olive oil

90 g (3 oz) chopped Brazil nuts, plus 6 whole shelled nuts

30 g (1 oz) chopped spring onion

120 g (4 oz) long-grain rice

3 tablespoons chopped fresh parsley

freshly ground black pepper to taste

Serves 6.

Preparation time: 1 hour 15 minutes.

Preheat the oven to 180°C (350°F or gas mark 4).

Lightly oil a baking dish just large enough to hold the tomatoes. Cut the stem end from each tomato. Carefully scrape out the seeds and pulp.

Salt the insides of the tomatoes and invert them on paper towels to drain.

In a small saucepan, bring the chicken broth to a boil, remove from the heat and add the saffron and set aside.

Heat the olive oil in a 1-litre (1-quart) saucepan over medium-high heat and sauté the chopped Brazil nuts, stirring often, until lightly browned, about 1 to 2 minutes. Remove with a slotted spoon to paper towels to drain.

Sauté the spring onion in the same oil over medium heat for 1 minute. Add the rice and sauté for a moment, stirring constantly Add the broth and bring to a boil. Then cover the pan and simmer for 15 to 20 minutes, until all the liquid is absorbed.

Mix the chopped nuts, parsley and pepper into the cooked rice. Stuff each tomato with the rice mixture and top each with one of the whole Brazil nuts. Place the tomatoes in the prepared baking dish. Bake for 25 minutes. Serve warm or at room temperature.

ORZO WITH PANCETTA AND PINE NUTS

120 g (4 oz) pancetta (other unsmoked bacon may be substituted)

2 tablespoons olive oil

90 g (3 oz) pine nuts

150 g (5 oz) orzo

500 ml (1 pint) chicken stock

1^1/$_2$ teaspoons chopped fresh oregano leaves (or ^{1}/$_2$ teaspoon dried)

salt and freshly ground black pepper to taste

Chop the pancetta and sauté it in the olive oil in a medium-size saucepan over medium heat until lightly browned. Remove with a slotted spoon to kitchen paper to drain.

Add the pine nuts to the saucepan and sauté, stirring constantly until browned, about 1 to 2 minutes. Remove with a slotted spoon to kitchen paper to drain. Add the orzo to the pan and sauté for about 1 minute, stirring constantly

Add the stock, oregano, salt and pepper, then bring the mixture to a boil. Lower the heat, cover the saucepan and simmer for 12 to 14 minutes, until all the stock is absorbed. Remove the saucepan from the heat.

Return the pancetta and pine nuts to the saucepan. Toss and serve.

Serves 4.

Preparation time: 30 minutes.

BARLEY WITH WILD MUSHROOMS AND CHESTNUTS

225 g (8 oz) chestnuts, shelled and peeled

1 tablespoon olive oil

120 g (4 oz) fresh wild mushrooms, such as chanterelles, shitake, morels or oyster, stems removed, sliced

45 g (1^1/$_2$ oz) unsalted butter

2 large spring onions, minced

60 g (2 oz) chopped carrot

60 g (2 oz) chopped celery

4 tablespoons dry vermouth

175 g (6 oz) pearl barley

1^1/$_2$ teaspoons chopped fresh thyme leaves (or ^{1}/$_2$ teaspoon dried) 875 ml (1^1/$_2$ pints) rich chicken stock, boiling

Preheat the oven to 180ºC (350ºF or gas 4).

Slice the chestnuts and set aside.

Heat the oil in a flameproof 2- or 3-litre (3^1/$_2$- or 5^1/$_4$-pint) casserole with a lid over medium-high heat. Sauté the mushrooms until lightly browned (about 4 to 5 minutes). Remove and put to one side. Lower the heat to medium, add the butter, spring onions, carrot and celery and sauté until the spring onions are translucent, about 3 to 5 minutes. Add the vermouth, raise the heat and bring the liquid to a boil. Add the barley, thyme and boiling stock. Cover and bake for 45 minutes. Remove from the oven, stir, replace the cover and let sit for 5 minutes before serving.

Serves 8.

Preparation time: 1 hour.

SWEET POTATOES WITH BOURBON AND PECANS

60 g (2 oz) unsalted butter 675 g (1¹/₂ lb) sweet potatoes, peeled and cut into 1-cm (¹/₂-inch) cubes

125 ml (4 fl oz) bourbon whisky

30 g (1 oz) granulated sugar

2 tablespoons fresh lemon juice

salt and freshly ground black pepper to taste

120 g (4 oz) coarsely chopped roasted pecans

In a large frying pan, melt the butter over medium-high heat and sauté the sweet potatoes, stirring constantly for about 5 minutes. Stir in the remaining ingredients, cover the frying pan, lower the heat and simmer for 5 minutes more. Remove the lid, raise the heat to medium and cook until the liquid is almost all gone, stirring often. Serve at once.

Serves 4 to 6.

Preparation time: 20 minutes.

THREE

MAIN

COURSES

LAMB IN MACADAMIA CREAM SAUCE

150 g (5 oz) macadamia nuts

2 medium-size onions, each cut into 16 pieces

30 g (1 oz) chopped fresh ginger

175 g (6 oz) plain yoghurt

2 tablespoons ground coriander

1 tablespoon ground cardamom

1 teaspoon freshly ground black pepper

250 ml ($\frac{1}{2}$ pint) thick cream

90 g (3 oz) raisins

1.25 kg (2$\frac{1}{2}$ lbs) boneless leg of lamb, trimmed of all fat and cut into 3-cm (1$\frac{1}{2}$-inch) cubes

salt to taste

chopped cilantro or parsley leaves for garnish

With a sharp knife, thinly slice 30 g (1 oz) of the macadamia nuts. Don't worry if pieces crumble; ideally, however, they should resemble shaved chocolate. Refrigerate in an airtight container until needed.

Place the remaining 120 g (4 oz) of nuts in a blender or food processor fitted with a steel blade along with the onions, ginger and yoghurt. Process, stopping to scrape the bowl occasionally until the mixture resembles porridge.

Place the purée in a large, heavy saucepan or frying pan along with the coriander, cardamom, pepper, thick cream, raisins and lamb. Bring to a simmer over medium heat. Lower the heat, cover and simmer for 1 hour 30 minutes, stirring gently often during cooking to prevent sticking.

Uncover, add salt to taste and raise the heat slightly. Continue to simmer for 30 to 45 minutes more, until the meat is very tender and the sauce has thickened. This dish is best made early in the day and allowed to mellow at room temperature, then reheated gently. Or it may be made a day in advance and refrigerated before reheating.

Serve with rice if desired, garnished with the reserved sliced macadamias and the chopped cilantro or parsley.

Serves 6 to 8.

Preparation time: 2 hours 30 minutes.

HAZELNUT STROGANOFF

60 g (2 oz) unsalted butter

675 g (1¹/₂ lbs) beef fillet or boned porterhouse, trimmed of all fat and cut into 5- x 1-cm (2- x ¹/₂-inch) strips

1 medium-size onion, halved and thinly sliced

15 g (¹/₂ oz) unbleached plain flour

1 teaspoon Dijon mustard

250 ml (8 fl oz) beef stock

90 g (3 oz) sour cream

150 g (5 oz) shelled, roasted and peeled hazelnuts

coarsely ground salt and freshly ground black pepper to taste

Serves 6.

Preparation time: 30 minutes.

In a heavy frying pan, heat 15 g (¹/₂ oz) of the butter over high heat and add half the meat, stirring constantly until lightly browned, about 1 to 2 minutes. Pour the meat and butter into a bowl.

Place another 15 g (¹/₂ oz) of the butter in the frying pan and repeat the procedure with the rest of the meat. When all the meat is in the bowl, add the remaining 30 g (1 oz) butter to the skillet and lower the heat to medium. Sauté the onion, stirring frequently until tender, about 5 minutes.

Add the flour to the onion and mix well. Add the mustard and then the stock and stir constantly until the mixture thickens slightly, about 5 to 7 minutes. Stir in the sour cream, half the hazelnuts, the reserved meat and the salt and pepper.

Heat over low heat, stirring often, until heated through. Do not boil.

Serve as is or over rice or pasta, garnished with the remaining hazelnuts.

TAGLIATELLE WITH CHESTNUTS AND SAUSAGE

30 g (12 oz) fresh chestnuts, roasted, shelled and peeled

750 ml (1¼ pints) chicken stock

1 small bay leaf

1 whole clove

1 small spring onion, peeled

½ teaspoon ground cardamom

250 ml (½ pint) thick cream

225 g (8 oz) spicy Italian sausage

500 g (1 lb) tagliatelle

30 g (1 oz) unsalted butter, melted

15 g (½ oz) chopped fresh parsley

freshly ground black pepper to taste

Serves 4 to 6.

Preparation time: 1 hour

Place the chestnuts, stock, bay leaf, clove and spring onion in a small saucepan. Bring the stock to a boil, cover and reduce the heat. Simmer for 35 to 40 minutes, until the chestnuts are very tender. Remove the bay leaf and clove. Place the chestnuts and spring onion with about half the stock in the bowl of a blender or food processor fitted with a steel blade. Process, scraping down the sides of the bowl several times, until the mixture is thick and smooth. Add the remaining stock, cardamom and cream and process until smooth and well combined. (The sauce can be made in advance to this point and refrigerated.)

Place the mixture in a saucepan and heat over low heat until steaming.

Heat a medium-size frying pan over medium-high heat. Cut the casings off the sausage and crumble it into the pan. Sauté, continuing to break the sausage apart with a spoon, until browned. Remove with a slotted spoon to paper towels to drain. Reserve.

Prepare the tagliatelle according to the package directions, cooking until *al dente*. Drain. Toss it with the melted butter.

Arrange the pasta on plates or a serving platter and top with the sauce. Then scatter the sausage and parsley on top. Add pepper to taste.

GRILLED SALMON ON COCONUT CABBAGE

6 salmon steaks (about 175 g [6 oz] each)

750 ml (1¼ pints) coconut milk

2 tablespoons fresh lime juice

3 tablespoons olive oil

1 large onion, halved and thinly sliced

1 teaspoon crushed red pepper flakes

1/2 teaspoon ground ginger

1 small head of green cabbage (about 1.3 kg [2½ lbs])

salt and freshly ground black pepper to taste

60 g (2 oz) shredded fresh coconut

Serves 6.

Preparation time: 1 hour 10 minutes.

Place the salmon steaks in a dish or pan just large enough to hold them. Combine 250 ml (8 fl oz) of the coconut milk with 1 tablespoon of the lime juice and pour the mixture over the steaks. Marinate in refrigerator for 1 hour. In a 30-cm (12-inch) sauté pan or frying pan, heat the olive oil over medium heat. Add the onion, crushed red pepper and ginger and sauté, stirring frequently until the onion begins to brown, about 8 to 10 minutes.

Pull the outer leaves from the head of cabbage and discard. Quarter the cabbage, then trim away and discard most of the core. Thinly slice the cabbage quarters crossways.

Add the cabbage to the sauté pan in batches, about a cup at a time, cooking down as necessary and stirring well. Cover and lower the heat to medium-low. Cook for 5 minutes, then uncover the pan. The volume should have been reduced significantly. Continue to cook, uncovered, stirring often, until the cabbage is lightly browned and limp, about 15 to 20 minutes.

Add the remaining coconut milk and lime juice along with the salt and black pepper to taste. Set 15 g (½ oz) of the shredded coconut aside for garnish and add the rest to the pan, stirring well. Simmer, uncovered, stirring occasionally until the liquid is reduced to a creamy sauce, about 10 minutes. (The cabbage may be made to this point in advance and reheated slowly as the fish grills.)

Remove the salmon steaks from the marinade, reserving the marinade. Season the steaks with salt and pepper to taste. Cook over hot coals or under a grill, basting a couple of times with the reserved marinade, until the salmon turns a much paler colour about 3 to 5 minutes on each side.

Arrange the cabbage on serving plates or a large platter. Top with the salmon steaks. Garnish with sprinkles of the reserved coconut.

SCALLOPS WITH LEMON AND PISTACHIOS

60 g (2 oz) unsalted butter

30 g (1 oz) finely chopped spring onion

675 g (1½ lbs) scallops 4 tablespoons fresh lemon juice

90 g (3 oz) shelled, peeled and roasted pistachios

salt and freshly ground black pepper to taste

lemon slices for garnish (optional)

Melt the butter in a large frying pan over medium heat. Add the spring onion and scallops and sauté until the scallops are opaque, about 3 to 5 minutes. Add the lemon juice and pistachios. Toss to combine. Heat through and season to taste with salt and pepper. Serve garnished with lemon slices if desired.

Serves 4 to 6.

Preparation time: 10 minutes.

SPINACH FETTUCCINE WITH STILTON AND PECANS

2 teaspoons salt

450 g (1 lb) spinach fettuccine

100 ml (3 fl oz) olive oil

1 garlic clove, crushed

2 tablespoons balsamic vinegar

225 g (8 oz) Stilton cheese

salt and freshly ground black pepper to taste

150 g (5 oz) roasted pecan halves, broken into large pieces

Bring a large saucepan of water to a boil. Add the salt and the fettuccine and boil until *al dente* (approximately 1 to 3 minutes if fresh; according to package directions if dried).

At the same time, in a small saucepan or frying pan, heat the olive oil over medium-high heat. Add the garlic and sauté until the edges are brown, about 2 to 4 minutes. Remove the garlic and discard. Remove the oil from the heat.

When the fettuccine is al dente, drain it and return it to the large saucepan or place it in a bowl. Add the hot oil along with the vinegar. Toss to coat. Crumble the cheese over the mixture, add salt and pepper to taste and toss again to mix and to melt the cheese.

Divide the pasta among serving plates. Top with the pecans and serve.

Serves 4 to 6.

Preparation time: 25 minutes.

TURKEY WITH WALNUT MOLE SAUCE

2 large poblano or Anaheim chillies

3 tablespoons olive oil

1 large garlic clove, minced

150 g (5 oz) chopped onion

90 g (3 oz) chopped celery

60 g (2 oz) chopped carrot

1/2 teaspoon cayenne pepper

1/2 teaspoon ground cardamom

pinch of ground cloves

125 ml (4 fl oz) good-quality port wine

30 g (1 oz) unsweetened chocolate, chopped

310 ml (10 fl oz) chicken stock

salt and freshly ground black pepper to taste

1.2 kg (5 lb) turkey breast

120 g (5 oz) chopped walnuts

4 tablespoons chopped coriander

Serves 8 to 10.

Preparation time: 50 minutes, plus the time to cook the turkey.

Wash and dry the chillies. Over the flame of a gas burner or under a grill, char the skins of the chillies, turning them with tongs as they blacken. Wet 2 pieces of kitchen paper, squeeze them dry and unfold them. Lay one on the work top. Place the charred chillies on the kitchen roll, cover them with the second piece of kitchen paper and let them cool for a few minutes.

Uncover the chillies and scrape off the charred skins with the edge of a knife. Slice the chillies in half lengthways. Remove and discard the cores and seeds. Chop and set the chillies to one side. To make the mole sauce, heat the oil in a sauté pan over medium heat. Add the garlic and onion and sauté until the edges of the onion begin to turn golden, about 10 minutes. Add the celery and carrot and sauté, stirring often, for 2 more minutes. Add the cayenne, cardamom, cloves and reserved chillies and stir to combine. Add the port and raise the heat, stirring until all the liquid has evaporated. Add the chocolate, stirring to combine. Then add the stock and bring to a boil, stirring often. Lower the heat and simmer, uncovered, for 20 minutes or until the vegetables are tender. Purée this sauce in a blender or food processor fitted with a steel blade. Return it to the sauté pan or refrigerate it until serving time and reheat gently stirring often. Season to taste with salt and pepper

Roast, boil or sauté the turkey breast, whole or sliced, according to your preference. Serve each portion of turkey topped with the mole sauce and sprinkled with the walnuts and chopped coriander

CATFISH AMANDINE

4 catfish fillets (or fresh-water perch)
(about 175 g [6 oz] each)

125 ml (4 fl oz) milk

45 g (1½ oz) unbleached plain flour

¼ teaspoon salt

¼ teaspoon freshly ground black
pepper

60 g (2 oz) unsalted butter

90 g (3 oz) sliced almonds

1 tablespoon olive oil

4 tablespoons dry vermouth or dry
white wine

Soak the catfish or fresh-water perch fillets in the milk for 1 hour in the fridge. Drain and pat dry.

Combine the flour, salt and pepper. Dredge the fillets in the mixture and place them on a piece of greaseproof paper or plastic wrap. In a large, heavy frying pan, heat 15 g (½ oz) of the butter over medium heat. Add the almonds and sauté until golden brown, about 1 to 2 minutes, stirring frequently. Remove with a slotted spoon to kitchen paper to drain.

Add 30 g (1 oz) of butter and the olive oil to the frying pan and raise the heat to medium-high. Sauté the fish fillets until golden brown, about 2 to 3 minutes, then turn them over and sauté the other side for 2 to 3 minutes, until golden brown. Remove to a heated serving plate.

Wipe out the frying pan and add the last 15 g (½ oz) of butter and the vermouth or wine, stirring until thoroughly combined. Pour the sauce over the fillets. Sprinkle the almonds over the top. Serve hot.

Serves 4.

Preparation time: 1 hour 15 minutes.

PEANUT CHILLI

450 g (1 lb) roasted shelled peanuts

3 tablespoons peanut oil

150 g (5 oz) chopped onion

4 garlic cloves, chopped

150 g (5 oz) chopped green capsicum

150 g (5 oz) chopped celery

150 g (5 oz) chopped carrot

2 jalapeno or serrano chillies, seeded and chopped

2 tablespoons chilli powder

$^1/_2$ teaspoon cayenne pepper (or more to taste)

1 tablespoon ground cumin

2 tablespoons chopped fresh oregano (or 1 tablespoon dried)

2 tablespoons chopped fresh basil (or 1 tablespoon dried)

410 g (14 oz) fresh or canned peeled, seeded and chopped tomatoes with liquid

875 ml (1$^1/_2$ pints) chicken or vegetable stock

2 tablespoons molasses

salt and freshly ground black pepper to taste

shredded cheddar cheese or queso blanco

finely chopped coriander

Serves 6 to 8.

Preparation time: 1 hour

Place 60 g (2 oz) of the peanuts in a blender or food processor fitted with a steel blade and process very briefly pulsing on and off, until the nuts are coarsely chopped. Set aside.

Place the remaining nuts in the blender or food processor and process, pulsing on and off, until the nuts are very finely chopped and cling together in clumps. Set aside.

In a heavy 4-litre (7-pint) soup pan, heat the oil over medium-high heat. Add the onion and garlic and sauté for several minutes, stirring often, until the onion begins to look translucent. Add the capsicum, celery, carrot, and jalapeno or serrano chillies and sauté for 5 to 7 minutes more, stirring frequently. Add the chilli powder, cayenne, cumin, oregano and basil, stirring thoroughly to combine. Add the tomatoes, finely chopped peanuts, stock, and molasses. Bring to a boil, cover, lower the heat and simmer for 30 minutes. Salt and pepper to taste. Like all chilli, this is best made in advance and reheated slowly stirring frequently. Serve hot, garnished with shredded cheese, chopped coriander, and reserved coarsely chopped peanuts. Serve with rice if desired.

BASIL AND SUN-DRIED TOMATO PESTO WITH WALNUTS AND PINE NUTS

175 g (6 oz) fresh purple basil leaves, washed and dried

2 garlic cloves, crushed

30 g (1 oz) sun-dried tomatoes packed in olive oil, drained, patted dry and chopped

60 g (2 oz) shelled walnuts

60 g (2 oz) toasted pine nuts

125 ml (4 fl oz) extra-virgin olive oil

60 g (2 oz) grated Parmesan cheese

salt and freshly ground black pepper to taste

This recipe makes enough pesto sauce for 500 g (1 lb) of pasta. For variations, you may use it on chicken, in omelettes, or on bruschetta.

In the bowl of a blender or food processor fitted with a steel blade, combine the basil leaves, garlic, sun-dried tomatoes, walnuts and pine nuts. Process to chop the ingredients, stopping to scrape down the sides of the bowl. Turn the motor back on and add the olive oil in a thin stream. Once the oil is incorporated, stop the motor and add the cheese and salt and pepper to taste. Process again, just until combined.

Use the pesto immediately or refrigerate in an airtight container

Makes 150 g (5 oz).

Preparation time: 10 minutes.

STIR-FRIED VEAL WITH CASHEWS

675 g (1½ lbs) boneless veal loin, bottom round, sirloin or shoulder, trimmed of fat and cut into 2-cm (¾-inch) cubes

1 tablespoon cornstarch

1 large egg white

4 tablespoons peanut oil

120 g (4 oz) raw cashews

1 2.5-cm (1-inch) piece fresh ginger, finely chopped

3 shallots, sliced, white and green portions kept separate

½ red capsicum, cut into thin strips 3.5 cm (1½ inches) long

120 g (4 oz) snow peas, stalks and strings removed, halved diagonally

1 tablespoon dry sherry

1 teaspoon granulated sugar

½ teaspoon salt

1 teaspoon dark sesame oil (available at specialist shops and Asian markets)

Place the veal cubes in a small bowl. Add the cornstarch and toss to coat. Add the egg white and toss again. Let sit for 15 to 20 minutes.

Heat the peanut oil in a wok or large skillet over medium heat. When hot, add the cashews and fry them, stirring until they are lightly browned, about 2 to 3 minutes. Remove the nuts with a slotted spoon to kitchen paper to drain.

Raise the heat to medium-high and add the veal cubes, stir-frying until cooked through. Remove with a slotted spoon to a small bowl and set to one side.

Add the ginger and the white parts of the shallots to the oil and stir-fry for 1 minute. Add the capsicum and snow peas and stir-fry for 1 minute more. Add the veal, sherry, sugar and salt and toss to coat thoroughly about 1 minute. Add the cashews, sesame oil and green parts of the shallots, toss and serve.

Serve as is or over rice.

Serves 4 to 6.
Preparation time: 35 minutes.

FOUR
Salads

THAI-STYLE PEANUT SALAD

Salad:

1 head iceberg lettuce, washed and dried

90 g (3 oz) fresh mint leaves, washed, dried and coarsely chopped

90 g (3 oz) coriander leaves, washed, dried and coarsely chopped

118-cm (7-inch) cucumber, peeled, halved lengthways, seeded and thinly sliced

2 medium-size tomatoes, cut into thin wedges

350 g (12 oz) mung bean sprouts, rinsed and drained

1 medium-size red onion, thinly sliced

150 g (5 oz) roasted shelled peanuts coarsely chopped

Dressing:

5 tablespoons fresh lime juice

3 tablespoons fish sauce (available at specialist shops and Asian markets)

$1^1/_2$ teaspoons granulated sugar

1 teaspoon soy sauce

1 teaspoon red chilli paste (available at specialist shops and Asian markets)

1 garlic clove, minced

6 tablespoons peanut oil

salt and freshly ground black pepper to taste

Serves 4 to 6.

Preparation time: 15 minutes.

Tear the lettuce into pieces and arrange on a large platter or individual plates. Scatter the mint and coriander leaves over them. Scatter the cucumber slices over the leaves and arrange the tomato wedges around the edges. Pile the bean sprouts in the centre. Arrange the onion rings over the top. Sprinkle with the peanuts.

Combine the dressing ingredients in a jar and shake well. Drizzle over the salad and serve.

FENNEL, ORANGE AND ALMOND SALAD

2 medium-size fennel bulbs with feathery tops

2 oranges

2 shallots, thinly sliced

2 tablespoons fresh lemon juice

4 tablespoons almond or olive oil

1 tablespoon honey

salt and freshly ground black pepper to taste

90 g (3 oz) sliced toasted almonds

Serves 6 to 8.

Preparation time: 15 minutes.

Trim the bulbs of any blemishes and cut off the stems above the bulbs, reserving any feathery green leaves. Cut each bulb lengthways into quarters and cut out the hard core. Slice each quarter crossways into .5-cm- ($^{1}/_{4}$-inch) thick slices. Place them in a serving bowl.

Grate enough zest from the oranges to make 1 teaspoon. Set to one side.

Chop 3 tablespoons of the fennel tops. Set to one side.

Peel the oranges with a sharp paring knife, cutting through the peel and pith. just to the flesh at one end, and spiralling down and around as if peeling an apple. Insert the knife along the membranes between sections, separating and popping out the sections. Remove and discard any seeds and add the sections to the fennel. Sprinkle with the shallots and chill until serving time. When ready to serve, combine the lemon juice, oil, reserved zest, honey, salt and pepper in a small jar, cruet or bowl. Shake or whisk to blend. Toss the salad with the dressing and serve garnished with the nuts and reserved chopped fennel tops.

ENDIVE, FIG AND WALNUT SALAD

90 g (3 oz) chopped walnuts

6 tablespoons walnut oil

2 Belgian endives, leaves separated

60 g (2 oz) small sprouts, such as alfalfa or radish

4 fresh figs, thinly sliced crossways

2 shallots, thinly sliced

2 tablespoons balsamic vinegar

salt and freshly ground black pepper to taste

Serves 4.

preparation time: 15 minutes.

Toss the walnuts with 1 tablespoon of the walnut oil and sauté in a frying pan over medium heat for about 5 minutes, until lightly toasted. Remove with a slotted spoon to kitchen paper to drain. Leave any oil in the pan.

Arrange the endive leaves on 4 serving plates. Top with the sprouts. Scatter the fig slices over the sprouts. Top with the shallots and walnuts.

In a small bowl, combine the vinegar with the salt and pepper to taste. Add the walnut oil in the skillet to the remaining walnut oil and, while whisking, add it to the small bowl in a thin stream. Adjust seasoning to taste and drizzle over the salads. Serve at once.

MUSHROOM SALAD WITH PARMESAN AND PINE NUTS

1 garlic clove, crushed

225 g (8 oz) mushrooms, stalks trimmed flush with caps, caps thinly sliced

4 tablespoons extra-virgin olive oil

60 g (2 oz) pine nuts

2 tablespoons fresh lemon juice

1 tablespoon chopped fresh oregano (or 1^{1}/$_{2}$ teaspoons dried)

salt and freshly ground black pepper to taste

90 g (3 oz) fresh young Parmesan cheese red leaf lettuce leaves (optional)

Rub the inside of a salad bowl with the garlic clove. Discard the garlic. Add the sliced mushrooms to the bowl.

In a small frying pan, heat the olive oil over medium heat. Add the pine nuts and sauté until golden brown, about 2 to 3 minutes. Dump the nuts and oil into the salad bowl and toss to coat.

Add the lemon juice, oregano, salt and pepper. Toss thoroughly but gently for about 2 minutes. (The salad can be assembled to this point and refrigerated.) Using a vegetable peeler, shave paper-thin slices of Parmesan and break them into 2.5-cm (1-inch) pieces. Add them to the bowl, tossing gently to combine. Serve in the bowl or place the lettuce leaves on salad plates and mound the salad on the leaves.

Serves 4.

Preparation time: 20 minutes.

SMOKED CHICKEN, PINEAPPLE AND MACADAMIA SALAD

675 g (1¹/₂ lbs) boneless smoked chicken, cut into 1-cm (¹/₂-inch) cubes

150 g (5 oz) thinly sliced celery

1 medium-size fresh pineapple, peeled, cored and cut into bite-size pieces

120 g (4 oz) mayonnaise, preferably homemade

1¹/₂ teaspoons Dijon mustard

2 tablespoons raspberry or sherry vinegar

salt and freshly ground black pepper to taste

120 g (4 oz) coarsely chopped roasted macadamia nuts

celery leaves for garnish

In a salad or mixing bowl, combine the chicken, celery and pineapple.

In a small bowl, combine the remaining ingredients except the macadamia nuts and celery leaves. Toss with the ingredients in the larger bowl. Refrigerate until serving time.

Garnish with the nuts and celery leaves before serving.

Serves 6.

Preparation time: 5 minutes.

WILD RICE SALAD WITH APRICOTS AND PECANS

175 g (6 oz) wild rice 150 g (5 oz) moist dried apricots, thinly sliced

250 ml (8 fl oz) fresh orange juice

$^1/_2$ teaspoon salt

2 teaspoons fresh lemon juice

1 tablespoon minced spring onion

salt and freshly ground black pepper to taste

6 tablespoons extra-virgin olive oil

$^1/_4$ cup finely chopped parsley

150 g (5 oz) coarsely chopped roasted pecans

Rinse the rice, cover it with cold water and let it soak for 30 minutes.

Place the sliced apricots in a small bowl and pour the orange juice over them. Set aside.

Drain the rice. Bring 1 litre (1$^3/_4$ pints) of water to a boil in a medium-size saucepan. Add the salt and rice and return the water to a boil. Cover, lower the heat and simmer until the rice is tender but chewy, about 30 minutes. Drain the rice. Drain the apricots, reserving the juice, and add the apricots to the rice. Toss to combine.

In a small bowl, whisk 5 tablespoons of the reserved orange juice with the lemon juice, spring onion, salt and pepper. Whisk in the olive oil and toss the rice mixture with this dressing. Add the parsley and pecans and toss to combine thoroughly. Serve at room temperature.

Serves 6.

Preparation time: 1 hour 10 minutes.

CHESTNUT, DATE AND APPLE SALAD

450 g (1 lb) chestnuts, shelled and peeled

750 ml (1¼ pints) chicken stock

1 bay leaf

225 g (½ lb) pitted dates, halved

1 large red-skinned apple

1 large green-skinned apple

1 medium-size carrot, scraped and thinly sliced

3 shallots, sliced diagonally

1 garlic clove, minced

2 tablespoons fresh lemon juice

1½ teaspoons curry powder

salt and freshly ground black pepper to taste

6 tablespoons olive oil

Serves 6.

Preparation time: 1 hour

Place the chestnuts in a small saucepan with the stock and bay leaf. Bring to a simmer, cover and continue to simmer for 30 to 40 minutes or until the chestnuts are tender. Keep the heat low so the chestnuts don't fall apart. Allow them to cool in the cooking liquid. (Cooling can be hastened by setting the pan in a sink filled with 2.5 to 5 cm [1 or 2 inches] of cold water).

Drain the chestnuts and remove the bay leaf.

In a salad or mixing bowl, combine the chestnuts and dates. Without peeling, quarter, core and slice the apples and add them to the bowl along with the carrot and shallots.

In a small bowl, whisk together the garlic, lemon juice, curry powder, salt and pepper. Whisk in the olive oil and toss with the salad ingredients. Serve at once.

PRAWN SALAD WITH CASHEWS

450 g (1 lb) large raw prawns, shelled and deveined

4 tablespoons peanut or vegetable oil

1 teaspoon cayenne pepper

3 shallots, sliced diagonally

1 large red-skinned apple

4 tablespoons fresh lime juice

60 g (2 oz) loosely packed fresh mint leaves

60 g (2 oz) roasted cashews

red leaf lettuce leaves

Place the prawns in a bowl and toss with 1 tablespoon of the oil and the cayenne pepper. Cook the prawns over hot coals or under a grill, about 2 to 3 minutes per side, until they are firm and pink. (Placing the prawns on bamboo skewers will make them easier to handle.)

Place the grilled prawns in a bowl (removing them from the skewers if used). Add the shallots. Without peeling the apple, quarter and core it, then thinly slice it. Add it to the bowl. Combine the remaining oil with the lime juice and pour over the salad ingredients. Toss thoroughly to coat. Add the mint leaves and cashews and toss again. Serve on the lettuce leaves.

Serves 4 to 6.

Preparation time: 15 minutes.

MIXED GREEN SALAD WITH BRAZIL NUTS

1 large egg

1 garlic clove, crushed

$^1/_2$ teaspoon salt

3 tablespoons fresh lemon juice

1 teaspoon dry mustard

$^1/_4$ teaspoon Worcestershire sauce

1 tablespoon grated Parmesan cheese

freshly ground black pepper to taste

125 ml (4 fl oz) extra-virgin olive oil

120 g (4 oz) shelled and sliced Brazil nuts

450 g (1 lb) mixed salad greens (cos, rand, chicory curly endive, iceberg, watercress, mizumi, spinach, mustard, etc.), washed thoroughly, dried and torn into bite-size pieces, about 350 g (12oz)

Serves 4 to 6.

Preparation time: 25 minutes.

Slip the egg into a saucepan of boiling water for 1 minute. Remove and set aside.

In a salad or mixing bowl, mash together the garlic clove and salt with a fork until they are well puréed. Add the lemon juice, dry mustard, Worcestershire sauce, Parmesan, pepper and egg. Whisk thoroughly.

Heat the olive oil in a medium-size frying pan over medium-high heat, then add the Brazil nuts. Sauté them until they are golden brown, about 2 to 3 minutes. Remove the frying pan from the heat, remove the nuts with a slotted spoon and drain them on kitchen paper. Don't worry about any small pieces.

Whisk the dressing mixture again while adding the hot olive oil in a stream.

Add the greens to the bowl and toss thoroughly. Sprinkle with the reserved nuts, toss and serve.

CELERIAC AND HAZELNUT SLAW

3 tablespoons fresh lemon juice

30 g (1 oz) granulated sugar

450 g (1 lb) celeriac or celery root (about 8 cm [3¼ inches] in diameter)

1 small red-skinned apple

1 small carrot, scraped and shredded

125 ml (4 fl oz) sour cream or plain yoghurt

2 tablespoons prepared mustard

4 tablespoons hazelnut or olive oil

salt and freshly ground black pepper to taste

120 g (4 oz) chopped roasted hazelnuts

Serves 6 to 8.

Preparation time: 15 minutes, plus at least 2 hours to chill and 30 minutes at room temperature.

In a mixing bowl, combine the lemon juice and sugar and stir until the sugar is dissolved.

Working quickly to prevent discolouration, peel the celeriac with a paring knife or nonswivelling vegetable peeler (You wont be able to get every bit of peel out of every crack.) Using a food processor or hand grater, shred the celeriac and immediately toss with the sweetened lemon juice.

Without peeling it, core and shred the apple the same way. Then toss it with the celeriac. Add the carrot and toss to combine.

In a small bowl, combine the sour cream or yoghurt, mustard, oil, salt and pepper and whisk until smooth. Toss with the slaw ingredients, then cover and refrigerate for a couple of hours or overnight. Remove from the refrigerator 30 minutes before serving and sprinkle with the chopped hazelnuts.

FIVE
DESSERTS

Pine Nut Shortbread

120 g (4 oz) unsalted butter at room temperature

90 g (3 oz) firmly packed light brown sugar

225 g (8 oz) unbleached plain flour

pinch of salt

120 g (4 oz) pine nuts

Makes 2 dozen pieces.

Preparation time: 1 hour 30 minutes.

Preheat the oven to 160ºC (325ºF or gas 3).

In a large mixing bowl, cream together the butter and brown sugar until smooth making sure no lumps of sugar remain. Add the flour and salt and work them together until a smooth dough is formed.

Place a 30- x 42-cm (12- x 15-inch) piece of greaseproof paper on a baking tray and lightly flour it. With floured fingers, transfer the dough to the paper and pat it into a 22- x 30-cm (9- x 12-inch) rectangle. Scatter the pine nuts evenly over the surface and press them lightly into the dough so that the nuts are anchored. (Move any loose nuts around to open spaces.)

Cover the dough with plastic wrap or greaseproof paper and refrigerate for 30 to 45 minutes, until hardened. Uncover the dough and slide it, along with the underlying greaseproof paper onto a work top. With a sharp knife or pizza cutter, cut the dough into 3-cm (1½-inch) wide strips and then into 10-cm (4-inch) lengths.

Place the strips 3 cm (1½ inches) apart on a baking tray and bake for 25 to 30 minutes or until delicately browned. Cool the shortbread on the baking tray for 5 minutes, then use a spatula to remove it to racks to cool completely. Store in an airtight container.

Butterscotch and Macadamia Bars

120 g (4 oz) unbleached plain flour

60 g (2 oz) icing sugar mixture

60 g (2 oz) unsalted butter at room temperature

90 g (3 oz) unsalted butter, melted

90 g (3 oz) firmly packed dark brown sugar

1 teaspoon vanilla essence

1 large egg

450 g (1 lb) roasted macadamia nuts (page 13)

Makes 16 bars.

Preparation time: 1 hour

Preheat the oven to 180ºC (350ºF or gas 4). Grease a 20-cm (8-inch) square tin.

Sift the flour and icing sugar mixture together into a small bowl. With a pastry blender, 2 knives or floured fingers, blend in the 60 g (2 oz) of butter until the mixture looks like small crumbs. Pat this mixture into the bottom of the greased tin to form a crust.

Bake the crust for 17 to 20 minutes, until lightly browned at the edges. Remove it from the oven and set it on a wire rack.

Whisk together the melted butter, brown sugar and vanilla essence until no lumps remain. Whisk in the egg and beat until the mixture resembles pudding. Add the macadamias, stirring to coat thoroughly. Pour the mixture over the crust and spread out evenly.

Bake for approximately 25 minutes, until browned all over and puffed slightly in the centre. Cool completely before cutting with a sharp knife into 5-cm (2-inch) squares.

BRAZIL NUT TORTE WITH CHOCOLATE GANACHE

225 g (8 oz) shelled Brazil nuts

2 tablespoons cornstarch

200 ml (7 fl oz) granulated sugar

$^1/_4$ teaspoon salt

6 large eggs at room temperature, separated

$^1/_4$ teaspoon cream of tartar

12 shelled Brazil nuts for garnish (optional)

Chocolate Ganache:

225 g (8 oz) semisweet chocolate

500 ml (1 pint) thick cream

1 teaspoon vanilla essence

Serves 12.

Preparation time: 2 hours 30 minutes.

Preheat the oven to 180°C (350°F or gas 4).

Grease 3 20-cm (8-inch) round cake tins. Cut greaseproof paper rounds to fit the bottoms of the tins. Put them in and grease them as well.

Place the Brazil nuts and cornstarch in the bowl of a blender or food processor fitted with a steel blade and process, pulsing on and off, until the mixture resembles bread crumbs. Add the sugar and salt and continue to process until well combined.

In a large mixing bowl, beat the egg yolks until frothy. Add the ground nut mixture and stir together until well combined. Set aside.

Beat the egg whites until frothy. Add the cream of tartar and continue beating until the mixture holds stiff peaks. Fold $^1/_4$ of the egg whites into the nut and egg yolk mixture until well combined. Gently fold in the remaining egg whites until thoroughly combined.

Divide the batter equally among the 3 cake tins. Bake for 25 to 30 minutes, until the cakes are golden brown and spring back in the centre when touched.

Remove the cakes from the oven and cool for 15 minutes. Run a sharp knife around the edge of each tin. Turn the cakes onto racks and let them cool completely. Peel off the greaseproof paper. Meanwhile, in the top of a double boiler, combine the chocolate and 125 ml (4 fl oz) of the cream. Heat over simmering water, stirring frequently until the chocolate is almost melted. Remove from the heat and stir constantly until the chocolate is completely melted. Stir in vanilla essence and set aside and allow to cool to room temperature.

Chill a mixing bowl, a beater and the cream until the chocolate is at room temperature. Beat the remaining cream until beater marks begin to show. Add the chocolate mixture and continue to beat until soft peaks form when the beaters are raised.

Spread the ganache between the layers of the cake, around the sides, and the top. Garnish the cake with whole nuts if desired.

BITTERSWEET CHOCOLATE TART WITH PEANUT CRUST

120 g (4 oz) roasted shelled peanuts

150 g (5 oz) unbleached plain flour

60 g (2 oz) granulated sugar

1/4 teaspoon salt

165 g (5¼ oz) unsalted butter

3 tablespoons cold water

4 large eggs

350 g (12 oz) bittersweet or semisweet chocolate

whipped cream (optional)

chopped roasted peanuts for garnish (optional)

Serves 6 to 8.

Preparation time: 1 hour 30 minutes.

Place the peanuts, flour, sugar, salt and 45 g (1½ oz) of the butter in the bowl of a food processor fitted with a steel blade and process, pulsing on and off, until the mixture resembles coarse meal. With the motor still running, add the cold water all at once and continue processing until the mixture forms a ball or clumps together. (If it does not do so within 20 to 30 seconds, add another teaspoon of water).

Remove the dough, dust with flour, wrap in greaseproof paper and chill for 30 minutes.

Preheat the oven to 220°C (425°F or gas 7).

On a floured board or pastry cloth, roll out the dough to fit a 22.5-cm (9-inch) pie tin. (If the dough breaks or separates, just tear off a piece from the outer edge and press it into the crack.) Fold the dough in half and carefully lift into the pie tin. Unfold and press it into the tin. Cut off the overhang 1 cm (½ inch) from the edge of the tin. Use the scraps to repair any holes. (Dampen the scraps slightly if you have trouble getting them to stay in place.) Fold the 1-cm (½-inch) overhang under the edge of the tin and crimp.

Prick the dough all over with a fork and cover the crimped edges with foil strips to prevent browning. Bake in the bottom third of the oven for 10 minutes. Crack 1 egg, separating and reserving the yolk, and brush the crust with the egg white. Bake for 3 minutes more. Remove and cool on a wire rack. Remove the foil strips.

Lower the oven temperature to 180°C (350°F or gas 4).

Put enough water in a double boiler just to reach the top section when inserted. Place the remaining butter, cut into 2.5-cm (1-inch) cubes, and the chocolate, broken or cut into pieces, into the top of the double boiler. Bring the water to a boil over medium-high heat. When the water begins to boil, turn off the heat, cover the saucepan and leave it on the stove for 10 minutes. Uncover the saucepan and whisk the chocolate mixture until smooth. Remove the top part of the double boiler and set aside until just warm to the touch. Whisk in the eggs, including the reserved yolk, one at a time, beating well after each addition. Set aside.

Fill the baked crust with the chocolate mixture and bake for 20 to 25 minutes, until the filling is set and the crust is brown. Cool on a wire rack. Serve cold with whipped cream and chopped peanuts if desired, or refrigerate.

ALMOND SORBET

120 g (4 oz) sliced or chopped blanched almonds

120 g (4 oz) granulated sugar

500 ml (1 pint) water

1$\frac{1}{2}$ teaspoons gelatin

5 tablespoons light corn syrup

$\frac{1}{2}$ teaspoon almond essence

1 tablespoon fresh lemon juice

Makes approximately 750 ml (1$\frac{1}{4}$ pints).

Preparation time: 20 minutes, plus several hours to freeze.

In a blender or food processor fitted with a steel blade, grind the almonds with the sugar to a fine powder.

Bring half of the water to a boil in a small saucepan. Remove the saucepan from the heat. Add 125 ml (4 fl oz) of the boiling water to the almond powder and set aside for 10 minutes.

Process again, gradually adding the rest of the hot water.

Sprinkle the gelatin over the remaining cup of water in a small saucepan and set aside for 3 minutes to soften. Heat over low heat, stirring occasionally until the gelatin granules are completely dissolved. Remove from the heat and stir in the corn syrup, almond essence and lemon juice. Stir to combine. Add to the almond mixture.

Freeze in an ice cream maker according to the manufacturer's instructions or pour into ice cube trays and freeze. For the second method, early on the day of serving or even a day ahead, place half the frozen cubes in a blender or food processor fitted with a steel blade and process, pulsing on and off, until the cubes are broken and the mixture is smooth and creamy.

Pour the sorbet into a freezer-safe container. Repeat with the other cubes. Seal airtight and freeze until ready to serve.

COCONUT ICE CREAM

150 g (5 oz) granulated sugar

4 large egg yolks

500 ml (16 fl oz) coconut milk made using all milk

60 g (2 oz) grated fresh coconut

1 tablespoon fresh lemon juice

250 ml (8 fl oz) thick cream

Makes 1 litre (1$\frac{3}{4}$ pints).

Preparation time: 35 minutes, plus several hours to chill and freeze.

In the top of a double boiler over gently boiling water, combine the sugar and egg yolks and whisk vigorously for 2 minutes. Whisk in the coconut milk and grated coconut and reduce the heat to medium. Cook the mixture, stirring constantly for 8 to 10 minutes, until thickened slightly. Cool to room temperature. (Cooling can be hastened by pouring the mixture into a stainless-steel bowl and placing the bowl in a sink filled with 3 to 5 cm [1 to 2 inches] of cold water.)

Stir in the lemon juice, then the cream. Refrigerate until cold. Freeze in an ice cream freezer according to the manufacturer's instructions. Or freeze in ice-cube trays, processing in batches in food processor until smooth.

ESPRESSO AND HAZELNUT CHEESECAKE

300 g (10 oz) shelled, roasted and peeled hazelnuts

60 g (2 oz) unbleached plain flour

300 g (10 oz) granulated sugar

45 g (1½ oz) unsalted butter, melted

900 g (2 lbs) cream cheese at room temperature

4 large eggs at room temperature

4 tablespoons Frangelico liqueur (a hazelnut liqueur)

4 tablespoons instant espresso coffee powder

250 ml (½ pint) thick cream at room temperature

whole roasted hazelnuts for garnish (optional)

Serves 10 to 12.

Preparation time: 2 hours, plus several hours to chill and 1 hour at room temperature

Preheat the oven to 180ºC (350ºF or gas 4).

Generously grease a 22.5-cm (9-inch) springform tin. Set it in the centre of a 30-cm (12-inch) square of aluminium foil and fold up the sides. Set aside.

Place the hazelnuts, flour and 90 g (3 oz) of the granulated sugar in a blender or food processor fitted with a steel blade. Process, pulsing on and off, until the mixture resembles bread crumbs. Place the mixture in a small bowl, add the melted butter and mix until evenly moistened. Press the mixture into the bottom and halfway up the sides of the prepared tin. Bake for 10 minutes. Let cool to room temperature.

Meanwhile, in the large bowl of an electric mixer or by hand, beat the cream cheese at low speed until soft. Add the remaining sugar and beat on medium speed until light and fluffy. Add the eggs, one at a time, beating well after each addition.

In a small bowl, combine the Frangelico and espresso coffee powder. Stir to dissolve the powder. Add to the cheese mixture along with the cream. Beat until thoroughly combined.

Pour the cheese mixture into the cooled crust. Bake for 55 minutes, turn off the oven and let the cake sit undisturbed for 45 minutes more.

Remove the tin from the oven and allow the cake to cool completely. Refrigerate for several hours or overnight. Remove from the refrigerator at least an hour before serving. Garnish with whole hazelnuts if desired.

RASPBERRY-CASHEW CRISP

900 g (2 lbs) raspberries

120 g (4 oz) granulated sugar

1 tablespoon fresh lemon juice

4 tablespoons dry white wine

2 tablespoons raspberry liqueur, such as Framboise or Chambord

120 g (4 oz) unbleached plain flour

90 g (3 oz) firmly packed light brown sugar

90 g (3 oz) unsalted butter

60 g (2 oz) coarsely chopped roasted cashews

whipped cream or ice cream (optional)

Serves 4 to 6.

Preparation time: 1 hour

Preheat the oven to 180°C (350°F or gas 4).

Spread the raspberries evenly in the bottom of a 20-cm (8-inch) square tin and sprinkle them with the sugar. Combine the lemon juice, white wine and liqueur and drizzle evenly over the berries.

In a small bowl, combine the flour and brown sugar. Cut in the butter with a pastry blender, 2 knives or your fingers until the mixture resembles bread crumbs. Mix in the cashews and sprinkle the mixture over the raspberries.

Bake for 35 minutes or until lightly browned and bubbly. Cool for 10 to 15 minutes, serving while still warm, as is or with whipped cream or ice cream.

WHITE CHOCOLATE-PISTACHIO FUDGE

400 g (14 oz) granulated sugar

175 ml (6 fl oz) condensed milk

2 tablespoons fresh lemon juice

$^1/_4$ teaspoon salt

300 g (10 oz) good-quality white chocolate containing cocoa butter, chopped

1 teaspoon vanilla essence

150 g (5 oz) shelled, peeled and roasted pistachios

Makes 36 squares.

Preparation time: 1 hour 30 minutes.

Butter a 20-cm (8-inch) square baking tin.

Combine the sugar, milk, lemon juice and salt in a heavy 2-litre (3$^1/_2$-pint) saucepan. Place over medium-high heat and bring to a boil, stirring frequently. When the sugar has dissolved, reduce the heat to low and cook without stirring for about 20 to 30 minutes, until a small amount of the mixture dropped into cold water forms a soft ball. (Be sure to keep the heat on low, or the mixture will darken.)

Remove the saucepan from the heat. If any sugar crystals have formed on the sides of the saucepan, wipe them out with a moistened pastry brush. Add the white chocolate to the saucepan, but do not stir. Press the chocolate down lightly into the mixture. Allow the mixture to cool to 43ºC (110ºF) or until the saucepan feels lukewarm to the touch. Then add the vanilla essence and beat with a wooden spoon until the mixture is thickened and smooth and has lost its sheen. (It will be quite difficult to beat the mixture, but don't stop too soon.) Fold in the nuts and immediately scrape the fudge into the prepared tin or onto the prepared surface and spread evenly. Cool completely. Then, using a sharp knife, cut the fudge into 36 pieces about 3-cm (1$^1/_2$-inch) square. For very smooth, sharp cuts, cool the fudge in the refrigerator for 30 minutes before cutting. Store the fudge in an airtight container and serve at room temperature.

CHOCOLATE-CHESTNUT TRIFLE

1 300- to 350-g (10- or 12-oz) sponge cake, thawed if frozen

120 g (4 oz) seedless raspberry jam

120 g (4 oz) broken chocolate wafers or biscuits

250 ml (1/2 pint) marsala or cream sherry

205 g (7 oz) granulated sugar

240 ml (10 fl oz) water

675 g (1 1/2 lbs) chestnuts, shelled and peeled

2 1/2 teaspoons vanilla essence

255 g (9 oz) semisweet chocolate

milk

pinch of salt

3 large egg yolks

250 ml (1/2 pint) thick cream, well chilled

60 g (2 oz) icing sugar mixture

glacéed cherries for garnish (optional)

Serves 8 to 10.

Preparation time: 2 hours, plus several hours to set and chill.

Early on the day of serving, or 1 or 2 days before, slice the sponge cake into 1-cm (1/4-inch) slices and make sandwiches with the raspberry jam. Cut the sandwiches into 2.5-cm (1-inch) squares and place them in the bottom of a 3-litre (5 1/4-pint) glass bowl. Sprinkle the broken wafers over them and douse evenly with the marsala or sherry. Cover and refrigerate.

Chill a mixing bowl and beaters. Place the granulated sugar in a 1-litre (1 1/4-pint) saucepan with the water. Bring to a boil and boil for 5 minutes. Add the prepared chestnuts and 1 teaspoon of the vanilla essence and return to a boil. Lower the heat to a high simmer and cook, stirring often but gently for 15 to 20 minutes or until the chestnuts are tender. (Add a little more water if the chestnuts seem to be getting too dry). Remove from the heat and select 12 whole or nearly whole chestnuts from the pan; set them on greaseproof paper or plastic wrap to cool. Reserve. Cool the contents of the saucepan completely (placing the saucepan in a sink filled with 3 to 5 cm [1 to 2 inches] of cold water will speed cooling) and then spoon the chestnuts over the chilled biscuit and cake mixture. Cover and refrigerate. Finely chop 225 g (8 oz) of the chocolate and reserve. In a 1-litre (1 1/4 pint) saucepan over medium-high heat, bring the milk to the verge of boiling, stirring frequently. Add the chopped chocolate and salt and whisk until the chocolate is completely melted and the mixture is smooth and on the verge of boiling. Remove from the heat.

In a medium-size bowl, whisk the egg yolks briefly then, while whisking constantly pour the chocolate mixture gradually into the yolks. Add 3/4 teaspoon of the remaining vanilla essence. Cool to room temperature (placing the bowl in a sink filled with 3 to 5 cm (1 to 2 inches) of cold water will hasten cooling), then pour over the chestnuts in the bowl. Cover and refrigerate until set, about 30 to 45 minutes.

In the chilled bowl, using the chilled beaters, whip the cream until it forms soft peaks. Add the icing sugar mixture and the remaining 3/4 teaspoon vanilla essence and continue beating until stiff peaks form when the beaters are raised. Spoon or pipe the whipped cream over the chocolate custard.

Shave the remaining 30 g (1 oz) of chocolate with a sharp knife or grater and sprinkle it over the top of the whipped cream. Arrange the reserved whole chestnuts and the glacéed cherries, if desired, on top of the whipped cream and grated chocolate. Refrigerate for several hours or overnight.

This dish may be made 1 or 2 days in advance or over 2 to 3 days. When serving, spoon all the way through the layers for each portion.

ROASTED PECAN PIE

45 g (1½ oz) unsalted butter, softened

105 g (3½ oz) firmly packed soft dark brown sugar

¼ teaspoon salt

205 g (7 oz) corn syrup (light or dark)

2 large eggs

1 teaspoon vanilla essence

pinch of ground cinnamon

265 g (9 oz) roasted pecan halves

1 22.5-cm (9-inch) unbaked pie shell

Preheat the oven to 180°C (350°F or gas 4).

Cream the butter and brown sugar together until mixed. Add the salt and corn syrup and beat until smooth and well blended. Add the eggs, one at a time, beating after each addition. Add the vanilla essence and cinnamon and beat until frothy and well combined. Add the cooled pecans to the mixture. Mix well by hand.

Pour the mixture into the prepared pie shell and bake for 40 minutes or until puffed and set. Cool slightly before serving.

Serves 8.

Preparation time: 1 hour

RECIPE LIST

Grilled Salmon on Coconut Cabbage
66

Hazelnut and Honey Muffins
44

Hazelnut Stroganoff
60

Lamb in Macadamia Cream Sauce
62

Mixed Green Salad with Brazil Nuts
98

Mushroom Salad with Parmesan and
Pine Nuts
88

Basil and Sun-Dried Tomato Pesto with
Walnuts and Pine Nuts
78

Orzo with Pancetta and Pine Nuts
54

Peanut Butter Biscuits
42

Peanut Chilli
76

Pecan and Prosciutto Bread
46

Pine Nut Shortbread
104

Raspberry-Cashew Crisp
114

Roasted Pecan Pie
120

Scallops with Lemon and Pistachios
68

Prawn Salad with Cashews
96

Smoked Chicken, Pineapple and
Macadamia Salad
90

Spinach Fettucine with Stilton and
Pecans
70

Stir-Fried Veal with Cashews
80

Tagliatelle with Chestnuts and Sausages
64

Thai-Style Peanut Salad
84

Tomatoes Stuffed with Saffron Rice and
Brazil Nuts
52

Turkey with Walnut Mole Sauce
72

Vidalia Onions Stuffed with Apples and
Cashews
52

White Chocolate-Pistachio Fudge
116

Wild Rice Salad with Apricots and
Pecans
92

Sweet Potatoes with Bourbon and
Pecans
56

RECIPE LIST BY NUT

ALMOND

Almond Sorbet
110

Blueberry and Almond
Muffins
44

Catfish Amandine
74

Cold Noodles with Spicy
Almond Sauce
24

Cranberry-Almond Soup
36

Fennel, Orange and Almond
Salad
86

Brazil Nut

Brazil Nut Torte with
Chocolate Ganache
106

Mixed Green Salad with Brazil
Nuts
98

Tomatoes Stuffed with Saffron
Rice and Brazil Nuts
52

CASHEW

Raspberry-Cashew Crisp
114

Prawn Salad with Cashews
96

Stir-Fried Veal with Cashews
80

Vidalia Onions Stuffed with
Apples and Cashews
52

CHESTNUT

Barley with Wild Mushrooms
and Chestnuts
54

Braised Chestnuts with Onions
and Prunes
50

Chestnut, Date and Apple
Salad
94

Chocolate-Chestnut Trifle
118

Gingered Chestnut Soup
32

Tagliatelle with Chestnuts and
Sausages
64

COCONUT

Coconut Ice Cream
110

Coconut-Prawn Soup
34

Curried Corn and Coconut
Timbales
48

Grilled Salmon on Coconut
Cabbage
66

HAZELNUT

Borscht with Hazelnut Cream
38

Celeriac and Hazelnut Slaw
100

Espresso and Hazelnut
Cheesecake
112

Fresh Figs with Black Pepper
and Hazelnuts
26

PINE NUT

Mushroom Salad with
Parmesan and Pine Nuts
88

Basil and Sun-Dried Tomato
Pesto with Walnuts and Pine
Nuts
78

Orzo with Pancetta and Pine
Nuts
54

Pine Nut Shortbread
104

PISTACHIO

Chicken Liver and Pistachio
Paté
22

Date and Pistachio Scones
42

Scallops with Lemon and
Pistachios
68

White Chocolate-Pistachio
Fudge
116

WALNUT

Endive, Fig and Walnut Salad
86

Fried Walnut Polenta with
Gorgonzola Sauce
30

Basil and Sun-Dried Tomato
Pesto with Walnuts and Pine
Nuts
78

Turkey with Walnut Mole
Sauce
72

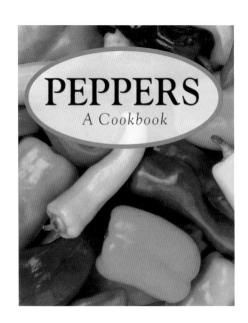

Simon Puttock

Horsey

Russell Julian

EGMONT

Ohe night, when the Baby was asleep, Moomoo-Cow said,
"Horsey, what do you like best?"
"I like the Baby best of course," said Horsey,
"and I like adventures, too."

"I like the Baby best as well," said Moomoo-Cow, "and I like kisses."
"Then give me a kiss, dear Moomoo-Cow!" said Horsey.
"Get along, Horsey," Moomoo-Cow giggled. "Don't be silly!
I only kiss the Baby. I couldn't kiss **you**!"

"But I **am** silly," said Horsey, "and I'll tell you what. If I can't have a kiss, let us have an adventure."

"Well, I've never had an adventure before," said Moomoo-Cow, "so yes, I **will**."

"And," said Horsey, "if you get frightened, you might need a kiss!"
"I won't be frightened a bit!" said Moomoo-Cow. "Let's go!"
So Moomoo-Cow and Horsey crept out into the . . .

. . . HALL!

"There," said Moomoo-Cow, "that was
a lovely adventure, Horsey. Let's go
back to the Baby now."

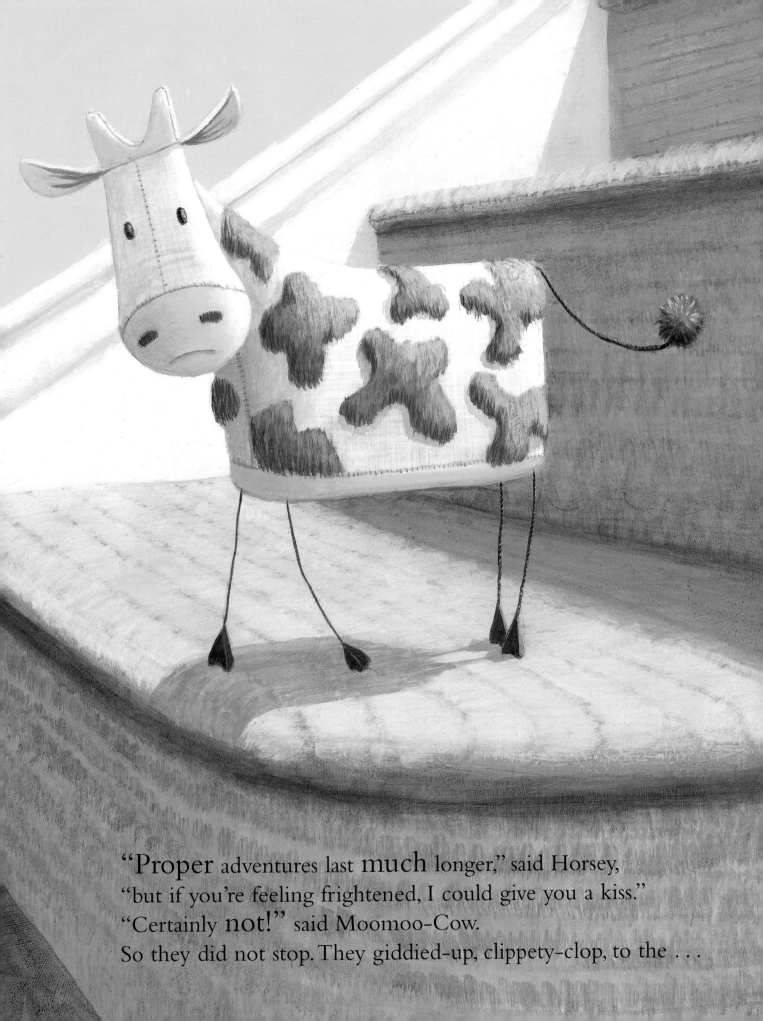

"Proper adventures last much longer," said Horsey,
"but if you're feeling frightened, I could give you a kiss."
"Certainly not!" said Moomoo-Cow.
So they did not stop. They giddied-up, clippety-clop, to the . . .

. . . FRONT DOOR!
"Horsey," said Moomoo-Cow, "everything's so big.
This adventure is too much. Let's go back to the Baby now."

"Proper adventures have to be big," said Horsey,
"but if you're feeling frightened, I could give you a kiss."
"Certainly not!" said Moomoo-Cow.
So they did not stop. They giddied-up, clippety-clop, to the . . .

. . . GARDEN!
And bang! The door slammed shut right behind them.
"Oh dear, oh dear," said Moomoo-Cow, "this adventure
is too loud. Let's go back to the Baby now."

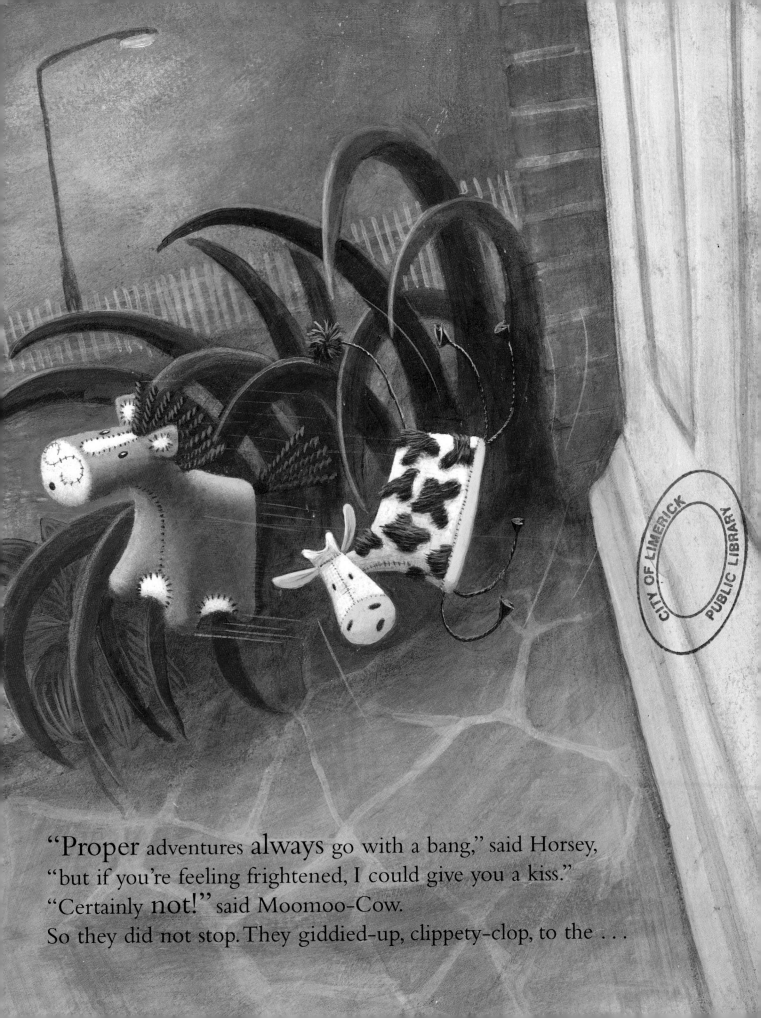

"Proper adventures always go with a bang," said Horsey,
"but if you're feeling frightened, I could give you a kiss."
"Certainly not!" said Moomoo-Cow.
So they did not stop. They giddied-up, clippety-clop, to the . . .

. . . GOLDFISH POND!

"Moomoo-Cow, do you think I'm bee-yoo-tiful?" said Horsey.
"You're bee-yoo-tiful in spots," said Moomoo-Cow. "But don't fall in, or this adventure will get too wet. Let's go back to the Baby now."

"Proper adventures are often wet," said Horsey,
"but if you're feeling frightened, I could give you a kiss."
"Certainly not!" said Moomoo-Cow.
So they did not stop. They giddied-up, clippety-clop,
until they came to the . . .

. . . BIG, WIDE ROAD!
An enormous car went vroom-vroom speeding by.
"Oooh!" said Moomoo-Cow. "That might squash me flat.
This adventure is too fast!"

"Proper adventures are always fast," said Horsey,
"but I shouldn't like you flat. I should be very sad,
and I would need a kiss . . . I don't suppose . . ."
"Certainly not!" said Moomoo-Cow.
So they did not stop. They giddied-up, clippety-clop, and then . . .

. . . the moon went and hid behind a cloud.

"Oh dear," said Moomoo-Cow. "Now this adventure is too dark."

"It is very dark," Horsey agreed.

"And we're far away from home!" said Moomoo-Cow.
"What if the Baby wakes? And what if the Baby misses us?
And what if the Baby cries? Let's not do any more adventure.
Let's go back to the Baby right now!"

"But Moomoo-Cow," said Horsey, "I'm feeling frightened,
and I need a kiss."

"Certainly not!" said Moomoo-Cow. "We will wait
for the moon, and go home."

And in a while, the moon crept out from behind the cloud. "Moomoo-Cow, the moon is back! The moon is back!" cried Horsey. "Let's not stop for anything. Let's giddy-up, giddy-up homeward!"

Moomoo-Cow and Horsey giddied-up and galloped all
the way home. Then they crept into the Baby's bed,
and the Baby woke up just that minute, and gave them
each a kiss and went right back to sleep.

"Horsey," said Moomoo-Cow, "we were just in time."
"Of course we were," said Horsey. "Proper adventures
always come out all right in the end. Did you like it,
dearest Moomoo-Cow?"

"I liked it in spots," said Moomoo-Cow. "But I wouldn't like another one again too soon."
"Oh, all right," said Horsey (feeling really rather glad).
"Sleep tight, Moomoo-Cow."
"Sleep tight, Horsey."

Moomoo-Cow waited until Horsey was asleep.
Then she gave him a kiss.
"Dear old, silly old Horsey," she said.
"Sweet dreams until morning."

Horsey, Horsey don't you stop,

The tail goes swish and the wheels go round,